Man o' War

THOROUGHBRED
Legends

Man o' War

Racehorse of the Century

E D W A R D   L .   B O W E N

ECLIPSE
PRESS

Essex, Connecticut

ECLIPSE
PRESS

An imprint of Globe Pequot, the trade division
of The Rowman & Littlefield Publishing Group, Inc.
4501 Forbes Blvd., Ste. 200
Lanham, MD 20706
www.rowman.com

Distributed by NATIONAL BOOK NETWORK

British Library Cataloguing in Publication Information available

Library of Congress Cataloging-in-Publication Data Available

ISBN 978-1-4930-6322-2 (paperback)
ISBN 978-1-4930-6497-7 (electronic)

♾™ The paper used in this publication meets the minimum requirements
of American National Standard for Information Sciences—Permanence of
Paper for Printed Library Materials, ANSI/NISO Z39.48-1992.

Man o' War

Contents

A Confluence of Destinies

Three decades after he bought the first racehorse he ever owned, Samuel D. Riddle bought the only racehorse he ever owned. The obvious factual contradiction in this statement does not negate the validity of its image. For once Samuel Doyle Riddle had bought into a master-servant relationship with Man o' War, the two would remain inseparable in the history, legend, and soul of Thoroughbred racing. That we may still ask at the dawn of another century, which was master and which was servant, seemingly would not offend Mr. Riddle, were he still of earthly environment and able to ponder the question with us.

Riddle apparently reveled in his joint identity with a flesh and bronze marvel bearing a name, and record, for the ages. This was not a matter of a man having in his lifetime one memorable horse, such as a Sam Rubin, who purchased and gloried in John Henry and, to date anyway, has taken under his wing no further star of the races. Sam Riddle not only bred and raced a series of important, glorious horses after Man o' War, but he did so with the genetic assistance of the great one himself. They even had noble names. Sons of Man o' War to carry the Riddle stable banner into the fray included Crusader, winner of a Belmont and two Suburban Handicaps; the swift War Relic and American Flag; and, finally, the Triple Crown winner War Admiral.

Heroes with heroic titles, they nonetheless could not diminish the tendency to say of Sam Riddle, whenever his name came up in the newspapers, "owner of Man o' War."

The avid outdoorsman and foxhunter himself helped burn this image into history with his pronouncement in the face of riches proffered as a purchase price: "Many men can have a million dollars, but only one can own Man o' War."

So, for the final three decades-plus of his life, Riddle flourished in the reflected glory of a horse. In this singular, and exalted, role he had been an active, aggressive force to be sure, but he also had been abetted by a wondrous libretto invoking fate, luck, timing, professionalism, legend, and poetry.

That Man o' War was even offered for sale as a yearling was a result of a complicated set of circumstances which embodied that most horrendous of human inventions — warfare — as well as one of its attendant, ennobling impulses — motivation to serve one's country.

Man o' War had been bred by August Belmont II, a titan of the Turf who had hardly made a career of raising his champions in order for them to bring glory to other stables. At the time Man o' War was a yearling, however, Belmont recognized the call of his country as it entered into the maelstrom known variously as "The Great War" and "The War to End All Wars." That it eventually would be pigeon-holed under the woeful name of "World War I" is sad testimony that it not only failed to end war, but, indeed, presaged even worse.

There was undoubtedly plenty of the "Over There" spirit of wartime songsmith George M.

Cohan inherent in Belmont's willingness, at the age of sixty-five, to accept a commission and an overseas post. That this deployment prompted thoughts about selling off his yearlings, however, was perhaps due in part to the nuisance of financial constriction, which had been a phenomenon unknown during most of Belmont's career.

At any rate, apparently after some waffling, August Belmont, the most powerful man on the American racing scene, at length decided to add what he suspected was a colt of unusual potential to that yearling consignment he had concluded should be sold in the summer of 1918. Riddle paid $5,000 for Man o' War, then saw him win twenty of twenty-one races and implant his name along with Red Grange, Jack Dempsey, and Babe Ruth among American sports icons of a nation's post-war crescendo.

Thereafter, the horse retired to Kentucky for a long and honorable career as a stallion, during which his dignified groom crooned his tales of greatness to so many audiences that legend and history merged into a loving and lovely litany.

The racing days of Man o' War were also those of

the Black Sox Scandal of the World Series, however. This reminder that even the Golden Age of Sports could not levitate above human nature is not without its connection to Man o' War. Since gambling is an ever-present element of sports, so great a figure as Man o' War might always be subject to those who wish to abuse him or traduce him. Where rumor ends and facts take hold was a riddle in the case of Man o' War. Dark rumors swirled about his only defeat, and his jockey in that event was, in fact, denied a license to ride, while tales linger of his trainer finding the stirrup leathers of Man o' War's saddle had been tampered with, as he stripped the animal after the final race of his life.

Indeed, such were the apparent possibilities, or paranoia, that there have been reports that Man o' War's owner had detectives watching over his own employee — Man o' War's trainer!

Whatever frailty, or avarice, or cynical suspicion might have lurked about him, however, Man o' War the animal was a creature of unsullied glamour and glory. As the sports writer Bob Considine rhapsodized, "He had a personality, and the dignity, of a

king. He was a great actor. Every race was a show for him and, like all great actors, he never let his public down." [1]

Edward L. Bowen

The Horse In A Gothic Arch

Abe Hewitt never forgot his first glimpse of Man o' War. "It was Futurity Day at Belmont Park," recalled the late raconteur, Thoroughbred breeder, and articulate observer of life. "In order to get a good look at Man o' War, we left the stands early. In those days, there were some large trees in the Belmont paddock, as well as clumps of laurel. Rounding some of the laurel bushes, one was flanked by tall trees whose branches nearly met overhead, like a gothic arch. Underneath this arch, framed by the dark shadows behind, stood a magnificent, copper-colored chestnut colt, with ears pricked. He radiated majesty, energy, and power — a veritable Alexander — awaiting the moment for new worlds to conquer. It was 55 years ago, and we never saw such a sight again." [1]

While Hewitt was no doubt aware that Alexander was a few centuries too early to stand under any Gothic arch, his point is eloquently made. Man o' War had an effect on those who gazed upon him and, if this syndrome were enhanced by his gathering glory on the racetrack, it did not depend upon his success altogether. Even when his future trainer, Louis Feustel, found him "gangly" as a yearling, the man felt a visceral stirring, a vague breath teasing out the guess that this might be a colt of exceptional merit.

Man o' War was, in fact, the ultimate in the lengthy breeding operation of the two August Belmonts. August Belmont II would not be denied the experience of watching Man o' War in action, or hearing praise for the marvel he had wrought. He would, however, be relegated to the sidelines, so frequently nettlesome in his advice to the real owner over what to do with the magnificent horse that his own wife was urged to shut him up.

The saga bearing the name of Belmont lingers in American racing, for the last and longest of the Triple Crown races is the Belmont Stakes and is raced at Belmont Park. The name was splashed onto the canvas of American sport by the father of the August Belmont who bred and sold Man o' War. This was August Belmont I, who was born in Germany in 1816 of

Jewish parents and, in one of those idylls of America's 19th Century, rose to stardom in finance and society.

Belmont was the son of a financier named Schonberg. As Abe Hewitt understood the name, "the first syllable means beautiful in German and 'berg' means mountain." [2] Thus, the name "Belmont" was a handy sobriquet to adopt when young August traveled to New York in 1837. He had already established himself as something of a prodigy in the Rothschild banking operation in Europe and, as so often is the case, engendered rumors that he was a "blood" Rothschild, albeit not a legitimate one.

Bernard Livingston, author of *Their Turf*, found Belmont a fascinating example of Jews rising in the social scene of New York. According to Livingston's telling, Belmont's original name had been Balmain, not Schonberg, and he had risen from sweeping floors in a Rothschild bank to representing the firm in the Papal Courts before bolting to America.

"With the funds of the world's largest private bank at his fingertips," Livingston wrote in one article, "he was important not only to industry, but to the United States Government, which was always running out of cash.

Belmont was short and rather stout, with iron-colored side whiskers, but there was something about him that attracted women...Men who had accepted his hospitality (at Delmonico's, etc.) began to say to their wives afterward, 'For God's sake, don't introduce that man to our daughters!' But New York society, for the next fifty years, would dance to whatever tune August Belmont chose to play." [3]

Among the "daughters" to whom Belmont was introduced, with or without the tremblings of their families, was Caroline Slidell Perry, whose father was renowned as a hero of the Mexican War and for his role in opening Japanese trade with the West. Livingston observed that, in addition to prestige, Commodore Perry's daughter had the advantage of being superbly turned out in a physical sense. (Given that this ultimately is the story of Man o' War, it seems that superior stature is a recurring theme.) Belmont married Caroline in 1848. They had six children, of which August II was the second eldest.

Belmont had become a wealthy man, but a conservative financier. Nevertheless, he became involved in helping revitalize the post-Civil War rendition of the

once flourishing national sport of Thoroughbred racing. In 1867, Belmont purchased the high-class horse
Glenelg. He later established Nursery Stud on Long
Island and then — being neither the first nor the last
to be seduced by tales of the benefits of limestone-rich
soil in Central Kentucky — he leased property between
Georgetown and Lexington. That, too, was given the
fundamental name of Nursery Stud.

August Belmont I raced a number of champions,
including Glenelg, Woodbine, Raceland, and Potomac.
By the time of his death in 1890, his son, August II,
had crowded into his business sphere and was fash-
ioning a career in which he developed a reputation for
being far more daring in a fiscal sense than the father.

August II purchased some of his horses from his
father's estate dispersal. Although the son would never
lead the owner's list for a year, as his father had done,
the mantle that was passed took on even more importance under the reign of the second.

That August II was more daring financially than his
father was summarized by Livingston in *Their Turf*:

"August Belmont II came into the picture when
rugged individualism was at its zenith in America...

Subways were being built, so Belmont hammered out New York's IRT. Canals were being constructed; he sliced out the Cape Cod waterway." [4]

In racing, Belmont was involved in the construction of the splendid Belmont Park, which opened in 1905 and became the site of the classic race named for his father. He also became chairman of The Jockey Club, as well as the New York racing commission, so that he might be seen as prosecutor, judge, and jury of matters coming before the racing industry. In those days, The Jockey Club not only controlled the registry of the Thoroughbred, but was looked upon to provide and enforce the rules of racing. When certain licensing and enforcement matters were passed on to the commission, Belmont might have to change hats, but not seats. For thirty years, he was the most powerful man in American Thoroughbred racing. Given subsequent decades' more conscientious adherence to democratic principles in this state-regulated industry, it is unlikely any one individual will ever again match his pervasive powers.

Ironically, Belmont's interests in a subway system in New York City put him in an adversarial relationship with another pillar of the Turf. This was William

Collins Whitney, who founded a dynasty which remains today through descendants and relatives by marriage. Around the turn of the last century, Whitney put in six years in racing before his death, and during this time, he and Belmont worked together to revitalize the racetrack in Saratoga Springs, New York.

Whitney had formed the Metropolitan Street Railway Company and, since this outfit had purchased most of the horse-drawn car lines, [5] the idea of moving masses of citizens underground had a competitive ring. Belmont took over the construction of the Interborough Rapid Transit Company and, by the time a demand had grown for a second line, Whitney had seen the light and successfully bid to build it. By 1906, the two firms had merged.

It was another bit of vision which might have influenced, indirectly and regrettably, the decision to sell Man o' War. Belmont "conceived the idea of building an eight-mile canal across Cape Cod that would shorten by seventy-five miles shipping routes from Boston to New York and avoid dangerous waters." [6]

This proved far more costly than original estimates, but Belmont stuck to it, allowing it to deplete his for-

tune to much less than it had been. In 1917, when the United States was drawn into World War I, he sought a commission and was posted to Spain with the Quartermaster Corps, procuring supplies for the American Expeditionary Forces. Such echelon of wartime service was in the family history, for August I had personally financed an entire Union regiment during the Civil War.

In 1918, it was apparent that Major Belmont's overseas stay would be prolonged, and he concluded it logical to sell his yearling crop. This was no small matter, for breeding and racing were of great personal importance to him. He was exceptional at the game, and in his life bred a total of 129 stakes winners.

At the time of his decision to sell yearlings, Belmont pondered which ones he might hold back. There were five fillies, four of them imports, that he kept, with an eye toward the future needs of his broodmare band. There was also a high-headed colt by Fair Play— Mahubah that had an appealing arrogance to match his long-legged energies. Belmont's instincts were brilliant, for the fillies all became stakes producers. Among them were Blue Glass, dam of Belmont Stakes winner

Hurryoff and Unbreakable (sire of Polynesian), and Quelle Chance, dam of Belmont Stakes winner Chance Shot and leading sire Chance Play. The colt which his horseman's instinct warned him to keep was none other than Man o' War. But in the end he decided to sell him.

Man o' War had been named by Mrs. Belmont, the former actress Eleanor Robson.

Sam Hildreth, the great trainer who worked for Belmont just prior to the advent of Man o' War, noted that Belmont had indeed intended to withhold the colt from sale, but was "afraid the entire sale might suffer if he made any reservations." [7]

During the summer leading to the sale of the Belmont yearlings, a draft, or drafts, of them were offered privately. Packages were offered at $30,000 and at $42,000, or thereabouts, but there were no takers. Louis Feustel, who would become the trainer of Man o' War, was quoted in a 1958 article in *Turf & Sport Digest* by Wayne Capps that he had been approached by Major Belmont's secretary, inquiring if Feustel's employer at the time, Sam Riddle, was interested in buying any yearlings. Feustel recalled that they were offered a dozen yearlings for $43,000. In an interview

with Arthur Daley of *The New York Times*, Feustel said that, since he had galloped the colt's sire, broken his grandsire, and trained his dam, he told Riddle: " 'I know all about these horses. Mr. Belmont always has three or four good ones every year. This is a bargain.' Mr. Riddle was interested and wanted to go 50-50 on the deal with Walter Jeffords (whose wife was Mrs. Riddle's niece). Jeffords sent his trainer, Mike Daly, to inspect them. He didn't like them. I begged Mr. Riddle to buy them himself. 'No,' he said. 'Mike Daly is more experienced than you. I'll string along with his opinion.' "

Fate might have been holding Feustel in her arms, assuming it was one chance to acquire Man o' War that slipped by, but not the last. On the other hand, the *Turf & Sport Digest* article did not completely square with the *Times* version and did not state point blank that Man o' War was in the draft of a dozen to which Feustel referred.

Whatever pushed Belmont over the edge, he wrote on July 24, 1918, to Mrs. Edward Kane, who was managing Nursery Stud: "As I already have notified you (by telegram), I have decided to add Man o' War to the sale..." [8] Since none of the package deals had moved, he would be selling at auction, at Saratoga in August.

Feustel was to remain a key figure in the unfolding scenario. As a youth, he had galloped Man o' War's ill-tempered grandsire, Hastings, and he had been an assistant around Man o' War's sire, Fair Play, when that noble horse was in the Belmont stable. He also had trained Man o' War's dam, Mahubah, so it had been natural that he would look upon horses of the Belmont breeding with special interest. Also, by 1918, Feustel had had a stint of training for Belmont himself, but was then working for Riddle, who was noticeably upgrading a racing operation that dated from the 1880s.

Conflicting stories have been passed down as to when Feustel first saw Man o' War. One version is that "he had inspected the colt at Nursery Stud (along with Daly) before he was shipped to Saratoga..." Years later, Feustel recalled that his impression of the colt was: "Very tall and gangling, he was so thin and so on the leg as to give the same ungainly impression one gets in seeing a week-old foal." [9] In various accounts, Feustel is said to have liked the colt immediately, although he was at pains to point out that he thought some of the other yearlings might be better.

It also has been told frequently that, after Feustel and fellow trainer Daly made their trek to Nursery

Stud to inspect the Belmont yearlings, they both reported to their employers that the horses seemed "undersized." The Belmont yearling crop was said to have been struck with distemper that summer, with Man o' War the last to overcome it.

Another possibility is that Feustel had not seen Man o' War before the colt was sent to Saratoga. As Hildreth's memoir tells it: "Later, when Mr. Belmont put them up for sale at Saratoga Springs, Mr. Riddle was struck with the appearance of Man o' War. He asked his trainers how they had come to consider that particular colt undersized and they told him that Man o' War had not been among the lot shown to them on their Kentucky visit. This made Mr. Riddle suspect that the owner of the Nursery Stud had in mind holding the Fair Play—Mahubah yearling out of the sale and also made him more anxious than ever to get hold of the youngster."

While it is easy to envision that Feustel's "gangly" comment would have been made in seeing a youngish colt, even if he did see Man o' War at Nursery Stud it was but a matter of weeks before he would see him at Saratoga. Perhaps that first impression came in August, rather than earlier; but, again, perhaps not.

Riddle, himself, also was quoted in slightly varying ways. This, of course, was a not unforeseeable circumstance given that human egos were involved and that the two men would be asked about the story countless times over the remaining decades of their lives.

The indefatigable research of Edward Hotaling, a journalist for NBC as well as racing historian, tells it this way: "The 21 yearlings arrived at the Spa (Saratoga) several days before the August 17, 1918, sale. The Riddles were ensconced in their large frame house at 215 (now 125) Union Avenue, a block from the track, and Sam, Louie (Feustel) and Mike (Daly) went up for another gander at Belmont's shipment. Sam agreed they were nothing special — until they reached the last stall. A big chestnut hovered in the shadows. 'Lead him out where I can see him,' Sam said, and he remembered later, 'He simply bowled me over...So I turned to Louie and Mikey and asked, 'What's the matter with this colt?' They said the Nursery hadn't shown them that one.' " [10]

The *New York Herald-Tribune* obituary of Riddle in 1951 is similar to the Hotaling and Hildreth versions, for it quotes Riddle as follows:

"You'll hear fifty persons tell how they influenced me to buy him, but don't believe them. I'll tell you. When August Belmont — the grandest man of the American turf — was selling his yearlings, I went down the stalls for a look. Red was last in the line, and I noticed he wasn't brushed and made ready like the others. I said to the groom, 'Mr. Belmont must have set this fellow aside,' and when Red poked his big head through the door my heart skipped a little...You see, I rode once and I've trained. I know them, if I do say it."

A little self-aggrandizement is certainly understandable, but Riddle may have either blushed, or harrumphed, had he been exposed to the Feustel *Turf & Sport Digest* article, in which the trainer recalled: "Man o' War went on the block late in the day, and Mr. Riddle didn't want to wait for him. But Mrs. Riddle saved the day by saying 'Louie wants him, and so I'm going to buy him,' and buy him she did." There is also the version that Mrs. Riddle's comment was "Louie likes him, and he's the one who's got to train him..."

(Abe Hewitt delighted in a story of when Riddle was around in person for Mrs. Riddle to one-up him a bit: "After Man o' War's prowess on the Turf had become legend, Riddle at times assumed airs of pomposity in reminiscence. One day, in the presence of his wife, who supplied most of the ready cash, he announced, 'The greatest day of my life was the day I bought Man o' War.' Mrs. Riddle cut him down to size: 'Sam, the greatest day in your life was the day you married me.' ") [11]

Riddle was a medium-sized mustachioed fellow variously described as "aristocratic," having the manner of an English general, and resembling an old Roman senator.

Yet another nuance on the purchase involves a tale that it was one James K. Maddux who picked out Man o' War for Riddle. Emily Hutchison, today one of the grand ladies of the Middleburg, Virginia, horse country, recalls foxhunting in Maddux' company as a child. ("We had a total of seventy-eight years between us. I was eight.") Maddux was an avid sportsman whose home, Neptune, in Warrenton, Virginia, burned one night on the occasion of a fancy-dress ball, which created the bizarre scene of his guests in odd costumes rushing about trying to put out the blaze. Mrs. Hutchison recalls that Maddux was one of Riddle's best friends and said it was commonly accepted in the area that Maddux had picked out Man o' War for Riddle. [12] Walter Vosburgh's

Racing in America (1866-1921), part of a series published by The Jockey Club, makes reference to Maddux, but is not specific on what role he might have played. The Vosburgh version conflicts with Feustel's recollection that Riddle did not wait around for the sale, while the Virginia tradition that Maddux selected the colt is at odds with Riddle's later assertions.

The noted Turf historian John Hervey, who used the pen name Salvator, authored a history of more than 200 type-written pages entitled *The Turf Career of Man o' War*. A copy was provided *The Blood-Horse* some years ago by well-known socialite and sportswoman Cee Zee Guest. In that manuscript, Hervey quotes Riddle at length, perhaps a bit naively allowing the owner his own bombastic spin. Hervey alleged that Maddux concurred that he should pay whatever price was necessary to buy the colt — $25,000 was mentioned. Riddle told Hervey that, once he had seen the yearling, "I couldn't think of anything but that colt after that. You know how it is when anything, especially a horse, just 'gets you.' That colt had taken possession of me. I already thought of him, in my own mind, as mine and I was in a fever until the sale would come...I hadn't decided how high I would go to get him. I just said to myself that I wouldn't stop bidding until he was mine. And when I got him for five thousand, it seemed too good to be true. I was too happy to contain myself."

What the record is clear on is that Man o' War was acquired for the Riddle account for $5,000 at the Saratoga sale on August 17, 1918. Exactly where is not so clear, however. At that time, the group of auctions that might collectively be referred to as "the Saratoga yearling sales" were a series of events conducted by two firms, Fasig-Tipton Company, which survives, and Powers-Hunter, which is seldom recalled in racing today. Various sales of individual consignors and groups of consignors were held during August in Saratoga in 1918, some in the daytime in the paddock of the racetrack and some at night at the Fasig-Tipton paddocks. In *American Race Horses* of 1947, distinguished co-authors J. A. Estes and Joe Palmer speak of Man o' War selling "under the Fasig-Tipton Company's hammer." Other versions concur, including *Man o' War* authors Page Cooper and Roger Treat's comment that Riddle inspected Man o' War as he "strolled about the Fasig-Tipton paddocks."

Conversely, a contemporary account in the August 24, 1918, issue of the weekly *Thoroughbred Record*, describes the scene as "an un-reserved sale of Major August Belmont's yearlings at public auction under the management of the Powers-Hunter Company at the racetrack paddock..." George Bain was reported as the auctioneer for the various sales under both banners and, anyway, since Fasig-Tipton became the surviving entity, there is sufficient veracity in interpreting its history as embracing collectively "the Saratoga sales."

Ed Buhler did the actual bidding on Man o' War, which might be read as supporting the version that Mrs. Riddle made the final call; a lady of that day might not have been comfortable brandishing her lorgnette — or whatever — in a bidding war. Buhler, whose business was manhole covers, was the uncle of the present day equine artist Richard Stone Reeves. Coincidentally, Reeves dates his own passion for the Turf from seeing Man o' War's son War Admiral win the Belmont Stakes of 1937.

Among the tales to have followed Man o' War's purchase is that Riddle thought him a likely hunter prospect. This may have been abetted by the fact that

Riddle from youth had been an avid passenger over the hunt field. Moreover, Robert Gerry also was said to have been interested in the big, rakish horse as a hunter prospect; the Gerry claim to be underbidder is more consistently supported than that of any of a number of other possible runners-up. (The Gerry family's descendants grew up hearing of the underbidder role. A granddaughter, Cornelia Harriman Gerry, once told the author that it was actually her grandmother who bid up to $4,500 on the colt but was dissuaded from going higher by her husband's declaration of "that's too much for a horse!")

As a hunter prospect, Man o' War undoubtedly would have been a high-priced number. At $5,000, he was certainly a bargain, but for his time and place he was hardly a "cheap" yearling purchase. Estes reported that the average price of yearlings sold at Saratoga that August was $1,107. Other versions consistently placed the figure at slightly less, $1,038, but given the disparity in qualities of consignments that were sold through the month it may be that not all parties included the same number of yearlings in their calculations. (The sales ranged from a major consignment from Claiborne Farm to a group

of nondescript French pedigrees that had escaped from wartime Europe.) Either figure puts Man o' War's price in perspective as hardly a bargain basement transaction. The top price of August was $15,600, paid for Golden Broom, who was to reappear in the Man o' War tale. Tops in the Belmont consignment was the colt Fair Gain, whom Joseph E. Widener purchased for $14,000.

The Thoroughbred Record account reported that, insofar as the Belmont sale alone was concerned, it involved twenty-one yearlings, which averaged $2,473; immediately under that article, however, the publication proceeded to list *twenty-two* yearlings as sold for an average of $2,375. Whichever figure is accurate, a gross of either $51,933 or $52,250 would indicate that Belmont's earlier packages had hardly been overpriced. (Prices dipped down to $200.)

Many, but not all, of the Belmont yearlings had been given names suggesting warfare, presumably by Mrs. Belmont. The former actress somehow had a feel for the military; the names ranged from the glorious (Man o' War) to the realistic (Drumfire, Battalion), to the mundane (Furlough, Sentry), to the grim (Trench Mortar, Tourniquet).

At odds with Riddle's quoted story that none of the Belmont yearlings impressed him much until he was "bowled over" by Man o' War, J. A. Estes reported in *The Blood-Horse* that Riddle bid on a far more expensive lot. This was Rouleau, a Tracery colt in the Belmont dispersal on whom the bidding reached $13,600 and finally was secured by Frank M. Taylor for Meadowbrook Stock Farm. Moreover, *The Thoroughbred Record* of November 30, 1918, commented that "No more enthusiastic sportsman has been seen than the master of Glen Riddle, nor has there been a more liberal patron of the sport of racing than he. At Saratoga, during the past two seasons, he has bought many of the highest priced and best bred yearling offers. His purchases of Thoroughbreds during the last five years amount to several hundred thousand dollars, and thus far he has not been rewarded for his generous outlay." If a $5,000 colt made his heart skip, some of his other purchases must have sent him into swoons of ecstasy!

As to what others thought of Man o' War, one bit of evidence which was saved was retold by Abe Hewitt in *Sire Lines*: Hewitt "once asked the late Max Hirsch and the late Col. Phil Chinn, who each enjoyed exceptional

reputations as judges of yearlings, why each one had not bought Man o' War for his own account."

Hirsch was the Hall of Fame trainer who later was the breeder of record of the champion Stymie, a high-headed charger inbred to Man o' War. He told Hewitt that Man o' War as a yearling that summer "was too nervous. He had pawed a deep trench in the dirt underneath the webbing of his stall door."

Chinn, a Kentucky horse trader to whom the phrase "caveat emptor" was the Eleventh Commandment, passed off the question with mock scorn of an element of the colt's pedigree: "His third dam was by MacGregor. That MacGregor crossed stopped me."

Hewitt assured his readers that this comment was followed by a chuckle and that Chinn in general had little knowledge of or interest in pedigrees. Nevertheless, there was a hint of acumen to the comment, for, while Man o' War was the scion of a proud and fashionable sire line, there were certainly elements of his female family which seemed ill cast for greatness.

MAN O' WAR

CHAPTER 2

A Passing Of Flaming Batons

Reliance on flame and fire for imagery was frequent in attempts to describe both Man o' War and his ancestry. The popular racing writer Joe Palmer likened Man o' War to "a living flame," while numerous variations upon the theme were affixed to the temperament and/or coat color of the horse, his sire, and grandsire — fire, flaming, fiery, molten, etc. In the case of his grandsire, Hastings, even this was not emotive enough for J. A. Estes, who addressed the issue in a poetic paean as "Hastings' wrath in his heart." [1]

Juxtaposed to such exaltation was the previous reputation of Man o' War's female family. In response to Man o' War's two-year-old season, England's *Bloodstock Breeders' Review* of 1919 remarked: "The line is anything but a distinguished one, and it is really astonishing that it should suddenly have gained notoriety as the result of Man o' War's superlative merits."

The Sire Line

Hastings was a son of the 1879 Belmont Stakes winner Spendthrift and was out of the distinguished mare Cinderella (by Tomahawk), she also the dam of 1898 Kentucky Derby winner Plaudit. Spendthrift was by Australian, a foundation stallion whose importation introduced the sire line to American shores around the time of the Civil War. Australian's sire, West Australian, in 1853 had become the first winner of England's Triple Crown — the Two Thousand Guineas, Epsom Derby, and St. Leger.

According to Abe Hewitt, Cinderella transmitted to Hastings an "overdose" of a "fiendish temper." [2]

Nevertheless, Hastings was a highly effective racehorse. August Belmont II paid $37,000 for him when he was a two-year-old in training in 1895. Presumably, Belmont harbored the thought that Hastings was a good thing for the Futurity Stakes, for when the colt finished fifth in that event several months later, Belmont reportedly had a bit of a row with trainer Andrew Jackson Joyner. The following year, in fact, Belmont's trainer was J. J. Hyland.

At three, Hastings found himself in a series of battles with a high-class crop including Ben Brush and Handspring. Hastings got in his best innings in winning the Toboggan against older horses and defeating Handspring by a nose in the one and three-eighths-mile Belmont Stakes. By season's end, he showed signs of going stale, and the following year his cantankerous personality was more pronounced. He reportedly made every aspect of training, from tacking up to breezing, a tribulation for all involved.

At one point, he came into the life of young Louis Feustel, and the related connections would be the bellwether of the young man's professional career. Born and raised on Long Island, not far from the original Nursery Stud, which had been established by August Belmont I, Feustel went to work there at the age of ten or eleven for $1 a day. [3] There Feustel and his brother were required to attend school and church as well as to work.

"The first horse I ever rode threw me one afternoon," he recalled, but "...I learned to ride fairly well. I was then

given the job of exercising a horse named Hastings, and I did pretty well until he ran away with me one day. We had covered two miles before I was able to stop him."

Despite being well known for such contretemps, Hastings added a notable campaign at four, when his natural speed was the focal point of his victories. These included a dead heat at six furlongs with the famed Clifford, a victory at five furlongs in :59 1/4, and a seven-furlong handicap score under 140 pounds. Just as Lord Derby's sprinter Phalaris would become a great stallion despite apparently being poorly cast in a breeding operation of classic winners, [4] Hastings the speed horse dominated over Hastings the Belmont winner in his career at stud.

Standing at Belmont's Nursery Stud in Kentucky, Hastings had strong competition in the stallion roster. He outstripped the stallion record of a more renowned Belmont purchase, Henry of Navarre, and also had competition for the farm's best mares from the English Triple Crown winner Rock Sand, who also was ensconced on the property. Hastings developed more of a reputation for siring successful two-year-olds than for stayers, and he led America's sire list twice, in 1902 and 1908.

In 1904, when Hastings was eleven, his book included the eight-year-old Fairy Gold, who had won the Woodcote Stakes, an important spring race for two-year-old fillies in England. Fairy Gold was by Bend Or, one of the most notable of stallions and the sire of the great, unbeaten English Triple Crown winner Ormonde. The resulting Hastings—Fairy Gold colt, foaled in 1905, was Fair Play. He was said by some historians to have been the best of the colts to carry the colors (scarlet silks, maroon sleeves, black cap) of his breeder, August Belmont II. On the contrary, the great trainer Sam Hildreth regarded Friar Rock, another among Fairy Gold's five stakes winners, to be the best colt he ever saw over the longer distances. [5]

Ironically, Fair Play contends for pride of place in the proud history of the Belmonts without even having been best, or second best, of his foal crop. The American foals of 1905 included James R. Keene's vaunted pair of Colin and Celt, foaled a few miles from Nursery Stud, at Keene's aristocratic Castleton Stud. Celt lost to nobody except Colin; Colin lost to nobody at all.

Fair Play made a number of runs at Colin. In the

midst of a promising, though not brilliant, two-year-old season, Fair Play won three of ten, and three of the seven defeats were at the hands of Colin. At three, Fair Play was better, but not good enough to defeat the undefeated. At a mile in the Withers Stakes, Colin beat him by two lengths. Then, in one of those races whose facts are merged — or submerged — in myth, they met again in the Belmont, then run at one and three-eighths miles. The tales surrounding that Belmont of 1908 include (a) Colin was bowed in both front tendons and (b) jockey Joe Notter misjudged the finish line. It is unlikely that a horseman such as James Rowe Sr. would run a horse with two bows, even more unlikely that such a battered warrior could win a race of that sort.

The fact that Colin ran once more after the Belmont also would indicate that, while he might indeed have been going lame, he was not an ambulance case on Belmont Day. Nonetheless, the likelihood is that all was not well with the unbeaten wonder, for, under the rules of the day that allowed late decisions as to starting a horse, it has been reported that trainer Rowe "conferred with Keene, and it was decided to make Colin an added starter." [6]

The question of Notter misjudging the finish seems more likely, although the little man denied it — why would he not? There was an extension beyond the usual finish line at Belmont for races of one and three-eighths miles at that time and the fact that Colin seemed to have a clear lead at the regular post and just held on to win by a head at the race's finish is intriguing.

On the other hand, the oppressive fog of the day was such that no earlier details or times of the race were recorded, so that even eyewitness accounts are suspect. Notter held that once he saw Fair Play coming, he asked Colin for more and the colt responded.

Colin was retired with fifteen wins in fifteen starts, and his back-up, Celt, defeated Fair Play while giving him eight pounds in the Brooklyn Handicap. Trainer Rowe clearly had Fair Play's number, but there would come a day when a son of Fair Play would set the great trainer's teeth into a prolonged grinding.

After Colin and Celt were retired, Fair Play generally found New York racing a more pleasant vista — although the Keene colors popped up to taunt him again when the older Ballot beat him in the Suburban. After the Belmont, Fair Play won seven of his remaining

eleven races at three, including the Brooklyn Derby, Lawrence Realization, and Jerome. In the one and one-quarter-mile First Special at Gravesend, he set a track record of 2:03 2/5 as the topweight. He also had set track records at four longer distances.

Reformists offended by gambling had cast a pall over racing in New York and numerous other states, and several of the better Eastern stables, including Belmont's, responded to the handwriting on the wall by repairing to England. There, the "Hastings" came out in Fair Play in no uncertain terms. He failed to place in six races and was said to have run decently only once, when fourth in the Coronation Cup. Belmont was willing to give up on him as an English racehorse, but was undeterred in his belief in Fair Play as a stallion prospect. Accordingly, the horse was sent to stud at Nursery with a career record of thirty-two starts, ten wins, and fourteen placings, as well as earnings of $86,950.

Among Belmont's spectacular investments in bloodstock had been the purchase of English Triple Crown winner Rock Sand for $125,000. That acquisition had been made in 1906, when Fair Play was a yearling.

Nonetheless, *Man o' War* authors Page Cooper and Roger Treat found a 1910 *Daily Racing Form* article in which Belmont was quoted as cheerleading for Fair Play as he was about to enter his first season at stud: "Fair Play is the best horse I have ever owned — I expect him to show by his get that he is the superior of his sire (Hastings), Rock Sand, Singleton, and all the other sires I have had."

It is worth remembering that Belmont represented an era when sportsmen had certain considerations in the breeding of their horses that no longer enter into Thoroughbred mating decisions. This was a lingering concern with producing sound, sturdy horses for society at large, especially in the realm of warfare.

Today, the phrase "improvement of the breed" seems an anachronism at best. It is as likely to be used tongue-in-cheek in reference to betting on horses as to represent any intellectually driven plan for the long-term genetic stewardship of a type of horse. Originally, however, improvement of the breed was a social goal that transcended sport, as when, in 1665, New York's Governor Nicholls declared that his establishing a race course on Long Island was

"not so much for the divertissement of youth as for encouraging the betterment of the improvement of the breed of horses, which through great neglect has been impaired."

Dorothy Ours, an employee of the National Museum of Racing in Saratoga Springs, has pursued a personal project of gathering material on Man o' War. She called to the attention of this author portions of a text she had found in the *New York Times* of 1911, in which Belmont was quoted in an impassioned plea for Thoroughbred racing and breeding to be recognized for its importance beyond sport and betting. [7] In 1911, the Turf was in the midst of a losing battle against Reformists, which saw racing in New York interrupted for two seasons. At a meeting of some 125 sportsmen in the Myrtle Room of the Waldorf Hotel, Belmont warned:

"The Army is beginning to complain that it cannot readily find horses required for the Cavalry. Think of it, in this vast country with its magnificent ranches and breeding farms, 500 horses each year for remounts are difficult to buy, and cost more than our Army officers find they should pay!

"...What would happen if in case of war, notwith-

standing a growing international desire for peace, if the
Cavalry had to be quadrupled, and instead of a good
Cavalry horse lasting ten years, as they do in time of
peace, the remounts of the Cavalry were lasting but
sixty days, which on good military authority I am told
is the average?..."

He continues that, because of their belief that the
race course is solely an institution for gambling, "the
misguided" moralists of the day are an "enemy to the
interests of our farmers, our ranchmen, military estab-
lishment, and all citizens who use and breed the horse
for pleasure."

In a particularly thought-provoking opinion in which
racing man and military realist seem to merge, Belmont
underscores that "...the entire system of stake and cup
races on the turf is framed to prove and test out the three
great qualities I have held up to you as cardinal and valu-
able: Endurance, early maturity, and courage."

From this distance, we must presume that "early maturity" was not construed to mean what it might today,
i. e., a two-year-old that can fly a solitary furlong in ten
seconds prior to a winter juvenile sale, or a five-furlong
star of April. Notwithstanding the importance of the

Belmont Futurity during most of Belmont's career in racing, his own breeding philosophy would seem to indicate that to him "early maturity" meant something more along the lines of a youngish horse able to withstand a hard gallop over a distance of ground.

The stud careers of the likes of Sir Barton and Omaha, or Belmont's own Henry of Navarre, might have languished insofar as siring winners, but they and other Thoroughbred stallions were certainly a major step up for most of the U.S. Army Remount mares that might be presented them. Hence, "improvement of the breed of horses."

At any rate, in Fair Play, Belmont indeed had a colt with stoutness as well as speed, and his faith in the young stallion was not misplaced. Fair Play led the American sire list three times, in 1920, 1924, and 1927. In twenty crops, he sired an average of thirteen foals annually for a total of 262 named offspring. Of these, forty-seven were stakes winners, an exceptional eighteen percent. In addition to Man o' War, they included Chance Play, Chance Shot, Chatterton, Display, Ladkin, Mad Hatter, Mad Play, and Stromboli.

(Ironically, because Fair Play went back to Alice

Carneal, dam of the great 19th Century stallion Lexington, he and Man o' War for some time would not be recognized as purebred Thoroughbreds insofar as the English General Stud Book was concerned. Alice Carneal was not considered a Thoroughbred. In 1913, strictures to prevent the wholesale importation of American stock to England, known as the Jersey Act, were enacted by England's Stud Book authorities. The Jersey Act was not rescinded until 1949.)

Reference has been made above to the emotive language which the line of Hastings-Fair Play-Man o' War induced. Among the best illustrations of what these horses did to the emotions of those who fell within their spell was a description of Fair Play by John Hervey:

"There was always something of a leaping flame about the son of Hastings and Fairy Gold, the effect of his flashing golden coat, his eager, agile movement, his disdain of familiarity, his lofty head and fiery spirit, unquenched to the last…Everything about Fair Play was balanced and proportionate and harmonious. It was the justness and poise of his physique which excited the admiration of the connoisseur."

A more personal testimonial came from one Peter A.

B. Widener II, whose father, the prominent racing man
Joseph E. Widener, was an associate of Man o' War's
owner, Samuel D. Riddle. In 1924, four years after Man
o' War's racing career had ended, the breeder, Major
Belmont, passed away. Soon thereafter, much of his
breeding stock was put up at auction, and Peter Widener
and his young bride accompanied his father to the auction where the family was to secure ownership of Fair
Play. It was a cathartic moment for Widener:

"Until after I was thirty, I was entirely indifferent
to racing…I had no time at all for this part of my in-
heritance. This hurt Father very much…It was a sore
point between us for many years. Today it is no longer
surprising to me that Father had two such different interests as racing and art. There is nature's own art in the
creation of the Thoroughbred. The flight of a filly and
colt across the countryside is a composite of all the arts.
It has motion and line and color…

"One afternoon, (Father) suggested that we accompany him to a horse sale…We went out of curiosity. We
came home with a new enthusiasm. The course of our
lives had been changed by a golden horse. The horse
was that grand old man of the American turf, Fair Play,

sire of Man o' War. I'll never forget him as he stood in the sale ring. The bright Kentucky sun streamed down upon him, burnishing his chestnut sides as if with gilt. He looked a king, and he acted more autocratically than any dictator. His was always a rebellious spirit. He bucked and kicked like any giddy yearling. Finally, he had to be led outside lest his too independent spirit injure an admiring crowd. The energy of the twenty-year-old horse, his royal impatience, got me. Then, too, it was a touching thing to see how well-loved he was. Members of the many families that had had a hand in the raising and training of Fair Play wept openly as the great horse was auctioned off. Tears streamed down the faces of old men and boys who had tended Fair Play in his 20 years of life." [8]

Such were the powers of the male ancestry of the horse named Man o' War.

The Female Family

Over the countless lunches the author had the pleasure of sharing with Abe Hewitt, many stories were told and retold. Among Hewitt's regrets was that during the period when August Belmont II on occasion would dine with the Hewitt family in their Gramercy Park home, the young Abram was under strictures as to children's discoursing with adult guests. Thus, he never had occasion to ask such a cheeky question of Belmont as, for example, "What on earth induced you to purchase Merry Token?" Inasmuch as Merry Token became the second dam of Man o' War, Belmont would undoubtedly have had at hand a response the young Hewitt might have learned from and put to good use. (As it were, Hewitt did breed a classic winner, Phalanx, in partnership with C. V. Whitney.)

Lacking any opportunity to pursue the question, Hewitt was left to write many years later in *Great Breeders and Their Methods*, "Why Belmont should have bought a mare of this class, sired by Merry Hampton — a proven failure as a sire — and whose first two dams were also sired by proven failures, is simply unknown to the author and is really beyond his comprehension."

Merry Token's dam was Mizpah, whose sire, MacGregor, was the element humorously flagged by Chinn as a reason to steer clear of Man o' War. Merry Token was the product of Broome Manor, the

Wiltshire, England, farm of E. J. Keylock, who generally kept three or four mares. Keylock's son, Major H. E.
Keylock, found a journal in which his father described
Merry Token's dam, Mizpah (the MacGregor filly) as a
selling filly (similar to American claiming status) who
on occasion was bid in for seventy-five pounds.

The elder Keylock purchased her for 150 pounds.
Merry Token was the fourth of Mizpah's five foals and
her get had made sufficient, albeit modest, strides up
the class ladder that the owner refused 1,000 pounds
for Mizpah two days before her death. [9]

Merry Token won a pair of five-furlong races at
two and a pair of mile races at three and was returned to the Broome Manor broodmare band. After
she had produced five foals, she was sold in 1902 to
Eugene Leigh, a successful international trainer, who
passed her on to Belmont. An early foal for her new
owner was Merry Task, an Octagon colt who was a
modest winner in England. (At the same time Merry
Token was sold, Keylock also sold off the mare Ulla,
a forty-guinea number who became the granddam of
Botafogo, arguably the "Man o' War of Argentina.")
In 1910, Merry Token produced her first foal by Rock

Sand, the 1903 English Triple Crown winner whom Belmont had purchased for $125,000 in 1906. This foal was named by Mrs. Belmont, as were many of the Belmont horses of that time. Mrs. Belmont recalled having heard the word Mahubah in Tunis, it being an Arabic greeting meaning "may good things be with you." [10]

The Rock Sand—Merry Token filly, thusly named Mahubah, was trained by Louis Feustel, who had worked for the Belmont stable in Hastings' time and had been foreman to Andrew Jackson Joyner during Fair Play's career. (Belmont changed trainers fairly often and it was not unknown for him to re-hire a trainer with whom he had once parted company.)

In 1908, Feustel had been hired to train a major division of thirty horses for Belmont. He was only twenty-four at the time and recalled years later that there had been some comment in newspapers with regards to his readiness for such a post. Early on, he scored a double at Pimlico, with the Belmonts in attendance, and "Mr. Belmont doubled my salary right on the spot to $150 a month."

In Mahubah, Belmont reportedly had a nervous

sort of filly, but Feustel did saddle her to win a single race from five starts. She was a dark bay, said to resemble her sire, Rock Sand, rather closely. Her debut at two came at Laurel on Oct. 10, 1912. Going five and one-half furlongs, Mahubah closed from ninth to be second. In the indifferent grammar of race charts, she "ran green…(then) finished with a rush." Despite that promising beginning, she failed to place in two subsequent juvenile races, at the Piping Rock meeting on Long Island and back at Laurel as a 3-5 shot.

Mahubah did not return until May 8, 1913, when Feustel sent her out at Pimlico to dominate a six-furlong race which she led all the way and won "in a canter" by three lengths. Winning "in a canter" would be routine for a certain son, but Mahubah was fifth of six in her only remaining race, a $500-added (but not named) event at Pimlico. She had earned $390.

Hewitt and other historians learned, or concluded, that Belmont had a number of standards for his breeding program: He favored matching sires and dams of different physical types, he shied away from sprinting strains, and he came to believe that hard racing was harmful for the potential of fillies as broodmare pros-

pects. This last tenet perhaps was a carry-over from experience with his great filly Beldame, who won twelve of fourteen races at three in 1904 and seventeen of thirty-one in three seasons, then was of little account as a broodmare.

Mahubah was not persevered with beyond her few races at two and three. Retired to Nursery Stud, she was, in essence, wedded for life to Fair Play, for all of her five foals were by the rising young star. (Most of the best of Fair Play's offspring were either out of Rock Sand mares or carried Rock Sand blood farther back. Rock Sand, sire of the English St. Leger winner Tracery as well as Friar Rock and others for Belmont, was resold to France because of the cessation of New York racing but died after serving one season there.)

The first Fair Play—Mahubah foal was Masda, a filly born in 1915. By the time Masda came along, Belmont had hired Sam Hildreth, a noted trainer he long had hoped to employ, but who hitherto had been unavailable. The young Feustel resigned, but said Belmont continued to pay him for a time, and he served a later stint again as the stable's trainer.

Hildreth's stay with Belmont lasted several years,

but before Man o' War emerged the trainer had left and had begun "organizing my own stable," he wrote. The Hildreth memoir recalled Masda fondly:

"If it hadn't been that I wanted to get horses in training instead of yearlings, Man o' War might have worn my own racing colors. I had handled Masda, his full sister, and I knew that if he possessed the same kind of speed she had he would be a humdinger. Several times when I had held the stop-watch on Masda she had run so fast that I thought there must be some mistake and I had asked others to verify what my own watch told me. But they caught her in the same time. In her works, she was one of the fastest tricks I've ever trained and she was good at actually racing, too, but not the same filly she was in the early morning gallops. I thought of Masda when I first heard of Man o' War, but I let it stop with thinking. Riddle didn't." [11]

Man o' War, the second of the Fair Play—Mahubah foals, was born on March 29, 1917, at Nursery Stud. The dam had had one barren year since Masda, who eventually became a moderate stakes winner and later an ancestress of Triple Crown winner Assault. [12] Following Man o' War, the subsequent full siblings

were Playfellow; the Jockey Club Gold Cup winner and successful sire My Play; and the moderate producer Mirabelle. Mahubah was barren continually after 1920. She lived until 1931 and in the interim was purchased by Joseph E. Widener, who also had acquired Fair Play and had a sentimental gratification in owning both the sire and dam of Man o' War. [13]

MAN O' WAR

CHAPTER 3

Timpani And Trumpets

A ll the magic and mystery and history delivered Man o' War to the stable of Louis Feustel, trainer for Samuel D. Riddle, in the late summer of 1918. In the modern context, a Saratoga sale yearling is presumed to be destined for a farm or training center. At the time of Man o' War, it was not unheard of for sale yearlings to be broken at the neighboring track. Considerable evidence suggests that there was little, or no, extra weight on the colt.

Feustel had the help of a former jockey, Harry Vititoe, in breaking the colt. Various reports indicate that the first saddling attempt might have been as soon as the day after the sale. Either that day, or at some other point in this rudimentary process, Vititoe was spilled by the big chestnut, who roamed about the Saratoga track area for perhaps fifteen minutes before being recovered. Feustel might well have thought back to his experience with Hastings and wondered if making such a point of associating himself with a grandson was such a good idea. The trainer was quoted to the effect that whenever he saddled Man o' War, he sensed that the youngster with otherwise acceptable demeanor must have reverted in his mind to that initial, disquieting experience. Certainly, if Man o' War indeed went from his accustomed halter and shank to being saddled and mounted in one quick lesson, it is no wonder that he reacted energetically.

In general, accounts of Man o' War as a youngster in training vary, and some tend to be suspect in that they were recorded years after the fact. The image of the horse as some heroic warrior no doubt colored both the questions, and the answers. Estes assured in 1947 that, after his unseating of Vititoe, the colt "gave very little trouble; though high-spirited, he was not quarrelsome." There were times, however, when Feustel had his foreman, George Conway, accompany Man o' War through the pre-race parade procedure all the way to the start. (Conway later trained two of Man o' War's best sons, Crusader and War Admiral, for Riddle.)

This description perhaps had insufficient masculine roughness for Riddle. In one edition of The Jockey Club series, *Racing in America (1866-1921)*, the historian and racing official Walter Vosburgh quoted Riddle that in the breaking process, "Man o' War fought like a tiger. He screamed with rage, and fought us so hard that it took several days before he could be handled with safety."

The Hervey manuscript provided *The Blood-Horse* quoted Riddle even more colorfully: "Did he fight? He did — like a tiger…No wild animal ever fought its captors more desperately…Once or twice, I really began to wonder just when and how it was going to end…What made him finally submit? Brains…"

Once the early scrimmages — of whatever dimension — were addressed, Man o' War apparently became tractable enough that he could be finessed through daily routines. Nevertheless, the nervous energy that Max Hirsch had described relative to the yearling pawing a trench in his stall was ever a part of the script.

"He was always on the bit," Feustel said, at least once, "always in a hurry. If I wanted him to walk, he wanted to jog. If I wanted him to jog, he wanted to gallop. No matter what I wanted, he wanted to go faster."

One of the difficulties in such a personality was that it extended to meals. Man o' War bolted his food, and, with his size and appetite, this was no small matter. He was said to weigh 640 pounds when weaned, the heaviest Nursery Stud foal of his crop, and the overly eager addressing of the feed bucket prompted Feustel to feed him with a bit in his mouth as a deterrent. Even so, there was at least one occasion when colic caused him to miss a race — if not an oat.

When autumn of his yearling days came, Feustel shipped the Riddle string down to winter training headquarters in Berlin, Maryland. Years later, *The Blood-Horse* reported Man o' War's stride at twenty-six feet, exceptionally long. In watching his burnished young warrior flaunt that stroke even as a stripling, Feustel began to muse that this might be something special in his life. Oddly, however, several events took place that tended to downgrade Man o' War, to the advantage of the flashy colt which had been the top price among all yearlings the previous August.

Kathleen Jeffords was the niece of Samuel D. Riddle's wife, Elizabeth. Her husband Walter Jeffords Sr. was a devotee of the Turf and would become one of its most distinguished pillars. The Jeffordses had purchased Golden Broom for $15,600 at Saratoga, and he, too, was wintering in Berlin. Mike Daly, who may or may not have seen Man o' War with Feustel on their trip to look over Nursery Stud yearlings of 1918, was the trainer of Golden Broom. In those days, head-to-head trials of yearlings were common, and there came a brisk Maryland morning when the white-legged Jeffords darling was tested against Man o' War. The distance was a quarter-mile, same as two-year-old races in the Aiken Trials of March today, and, at that short route and on that occasion, Golden Broom scooted off first and held on by a half-length. The high regard the Jeffordses had for the French-bred was surely enhanced by that. (Yeah, and my Little League coach said he once struck out Babe Ruth in an exhibition game.)

The above scenario has been repeated consistently so often that the author was stunned to read in the Hervey manuscript that Man o' War was tried against Golden Broom three times — at one, two, and three furlongs! Each time, the quicker starting colt held him off.

The preparing of a yearling-cum-two-year-old is an exercise in restraint and patience. At the same time,

the sapling must be tested, the complicated systems of organ, muscle, and bone set into purposeful ascendancy. The rakish young Man o' War had one setback in this pattern after being transferred from Berlin to one of the revered tracks in Maryland history, the long-defunct Havre de Grace. There he caught a fever, which reached 106 degrees. So captured and enraptured have been writers over the years that it has been a virtual chorus that all report his survival as the "fire of Fair Play outburning the fever," or something to that effect — underplaying a scary situation. ("Fire," of course, is so frequently prescribed as an antidote to fever.)

It was said that Man o' War was back at work a week later. As the winter gave way to spring, Feustel continued the preparation for competition, but there was no attempt to rush the colt. When the stable relocated to Pimlico, Man o' War was schooled from the starting barrier, which would not always be his friend. One of the great riders of the day, Johnny Loftus, who rode for Riddle, would come by some mornings to breeze the colt. Clyde Gordon was a regular exercise rider, Frank Loftus the groom, and Major Treat, a distinguished show horse from one of owner Sam Riddle's other equine pursuits, had been conscripted as a sort of partner and mentor of Man o' War. The Major's presence helped keep the fiery colt on the ground, and the distinguished old fellow sometimes went with him to the post.

Finally, the coming of spring had brought many of the top stables back to New York. Feustel was ready to send Man o' War into the fray. The colt had worked too well to be unknown, although he was said to have been edged by Dinna Care in a morning breeze that put on the finishing touches.

Man o' War made his first start on June 6, 1919, at Belmont Park. He was variously figured at from 3-5 to 1-5 against a field of six others going five furlongs on a straight course. Johnny Loftus was aboard. Man o' War broke well enough to be lapped on leader Retrieve during the first quarter-mile, continued to track that one for another two furlongs, then edged into the front and had a three-length lead. He continued to draw off, winning by six "cantering," as the *Daily Racing Form* chart called it. The time of :59 was 3 2/5 seconds off the track record.

Feustel, a large-framed man then in his thirties, perhaps pulled upon one of his cigars that afternoon with a frothy combination of relief, joy, and anticipation.

Three days later, Man o' War was out again. He was the prohibitive favorite for the five and a half-furlong Keene Memorial Stakes, again on the straight course of grand old Belmont. Soon the aura of Man o' War would suggest that the whole thrust of his strategy was to run horses off their feet from the beginning. However, just as he had stalked the pace in his debut, in the Keene he was second early to Ralco and then dropped back to third, two lengths behind the leader with My Laddie second after a half-mile. In the final furlong, Loftus got busy enough that the chart noted Man o' War "responded gamely to urging," and the high-headed chestnut drew off to win by three lengths from On Watch. His time of 1:05 3/5 was 1 4/5 seconds slower than the record for that straightaway. The track was listed as slow. Last of six was Mrs. Jeffords' Hoodwink, another whom Man o' War would see again. Already, there had been recognition that Man o' War was something over and above the general lot of sparkling two-year-olds. The *New York Times'* headline writer responded to the reporter's oceanic imagery. Under the headline "Man o' War Sails in As Easy Winner," the report reflected judgments that Man o' War already had been seen as the best two-year-old colt to have appeared that season. The reporter, or proofreaders, did not quite have the punctuation details of the colt's name down yet, but he was impressed: "…Man-o-War was a whirlwind, and from the eighth pole to the finish he was sifting along at forty knots an hour, with the others drifting behind him." The writer could hardly have known that he had just constructed a summary of the horse's entire career.

Man o' War exuded an aura that eventually prompted Feustel to proclaim: "He wasn't a horse. He was more of a deer."

Less than two weeks passed before New Yorkers could again check out the budding darling. On June 21, Man o' War appeared at the old egg-shaped Jamaica track for the five and a half-furlong Youthful Stakes.

In later years, the Youthful would be the vehicle for an early hint at stardom for the likes of El Chico, Native Dancer, and Bold Ruler, as well as hosting the first Affirmed win over Alydar. Man o' War's running was only the seventh, and he gave the race an early distinction. Carrying 120 pounds in a timid field of four, Man o' War again was favored heavily. He was more impressive than before.

Feustel had asked Loftus to school Man o' War at breaking and in the Youthful he virtually outbroke the old spring-up tape starting barrier then in effect and had a clear lead in the first quarter-mile. He opened four lengths in midstretch and coasted home by two and a half lengths over On Watch, to whom he conceded twelve pounds. The Riddle colt owned all the fractions, :23 1/5, :47 3/5, 1:00 1/5, and his final time of 1:06 3/5 was less than two seconds over the track record. (Owned by G. W. Loft, runner-up On Watch was a son of Colin, the unbeaten nemesis of Man o' War's sire.)

Only two days later, Man o' War came out again, this time for the twenty-ninth Hudson Stakes of five furlongs at Aqueduct. For the first time, Man o' War carried 130 pounds, an unheard of challenge for a two-year-old today but not in 1919. He opened at 1-10, despite giving from fifteen to twenty-one pounds to four rivals, including a Glen Riddle Farm stablemate, Rocking Horse.

Perhaps the effects of morning schooling in the art of the fast start had a downside, for Man o' War took his coach and passenger Loftus bursting through the barrier once in a false start before the Hudson. Brought back into line, he was "off in motion," an apparent redundancy by which the chart caller presumably was responding to something similar to beating the start. At any rate, Man o' War again led all the way, never opening much daylight as first Evergay and then Violet Tip tracked him, but winning in hand, by one and one-half lengths. The runner-up, Violet Tip, was the light-weight in the field, getting twenty-one pounds from Man o' War. The time was 1:01 3/5. (Rocking Horse rocked along in last place at the wire.)

Feustel had learned that a Man o' War quirk was the common horse trick of swelling up when being saddled, so he had to take extra care to walk along a few strides and gradually tighten the girth. For the most part, though, things apparently had been going in clockwork order until the colt's insistence on wolfing his food brought on a touch of colic, which caused him to miss the Great American Stakes.

This was a small inconvenience, for Feustel had him back a week later, on July 5, for Aqueduct's Tremont Stakes, his first run at as much as six furlongs. In a field of only three, Man o' War was heavily favored, again under 130 pounds and giving fifteen to Ralco and

eighteen to Ace of Aces. Man o' War and Loftus again broke alertly, took a length lead after a quarter-mile, and held sway by the same margin without squandering any needless energy. The time of 1:13 on a fast track was two seconds over the track record.

On August 2, one of the constancies of the Turf had come full circle, just as it does today. Approximately one year after appearing in the sale ring, the gaudy princeling was back on public display at Saratoga Springs, New York. This grand old Spa of human and horse had been prominent in American racing and society since the early 1860s, when visitors from North and South flung off their Civil War worries and settled in for some exhausting leisure and luxury.

Saratoga was a favored spot of Man o' War's owner, Samuel D. Riddle, and his wife. Riddle had been a "sportsman" all his life, and to him that word ranged from such fashionable pursuits as foxhunting, showing, and racing, to the manly art of raccoon hunting.

Ironically, one of the extant descriptions of Riddle was left us by J. K. M. Ross, whose father owned Sir Barton — the first Triple Crown winner whose path was to cross with Man o' War in an historic context:

"Mr. Riddle was very handsome. Every inch a gentleman, he resembled the classic retired British Army general in appearance and had a well-trimmed, military-type mustache to accentuate this illusion. Tall and very straight in his carriage, with a ruddy complexion which stamped him as a man who spent a great deal of time out of doors, he always gave the impression of extreme physical fitness. Throughout his life, he rode to hounds and…once described as 'Sam Riddle, who grins like a 'possum in that pleasing way of his,' he did, indeed, wear a smile well and often…

"Mr. Riddle and his gracious, soft-spoken wife owned a home near the racecourse at the far end of Union Avenue, and they entertained frequently, chiefly with a series of late afternoon parties. Almost invariably, they served mint juleps — perfect juleps in silver mugs thick with frost. At the mention of Mr. Riddle's name, I can still conjure up in my memory the exquisite taste and aroma of that indescribably delightful concoction which was the Riddle speciality." [1]

The thirty-sixth running of the United States Hotel Stakes at Saratoga brought out Man o' War, under his requisite 130 pounds. After a series of short fields,

there were nine set to oppose him. With that many youngsters milling about, the start was delayed for six minutes, after which Man o' War had the others questioning why they had bothered. He was in front by three lengths after a quarter-mile, edged out by four at one point, and sauntered home by two lengths. He had opened at 9-10 and action cramped the figure to 1-5. The fractions were all his and were brisk at :23, :47 1/5, and a final of 1:12 2/5. The track record was 1:10 2/5.

(Turf writer O'Neil Sevier commented in print that Man o' War was already a "veritable giant" and joked that Riddle was being teased about ringing in a four-year-old. He already topped sixteen hands "in his plates.")

Back in Fair Play's time, trainer James Rowe had held sway with Colin. The U.S. Hotel Stakes, however, found Rowe finishing second to Fair Play's son with a crack prospect from one of the prevalent stables of the day, that of Harry Payne Whitney. This was the colt Upset, who chased Man o' War home while receiving fifteen pounds from the budding star.

Eleven days later, they met again in the Sanford Stakes, and thereupon the history of Man o' War took on several of its many elements of mythology. Six romping triumphs had established an impression of burgeoning greatness about the big chestnut, but horse racing has a way of bringing reality home with a right cross or uppercut. Man o' War was beaten in the Sanford Memorial and thus presumably denied that extra cachet of retiring unbeaten, for he never lost again.

Few events in sports have been recalled as often as the 1919 Sanford Memorial. Over the years some constancy — or imitation — of recapitulation emerged, but much of it was probably exaggeration. Eventually, the fault was laid to Loftus, who despite being one of the crack riders of the day was said to have turned in such a bone-headed performance that the failure was linked with possible chicanery in some minds. The other villain was the substitute starter, who reportedly sprung the barrier while Man o' War was turned the wrong way.

The race which would go down in history for its unexpected result had shaped up prior to its unfolding as sufficiently enticing that the crowd was said to number about 20,000. In a field of seven going six furlongs, Man o' War was facing his old winter-quarters mate and presumed arch-rival, Golden Broom. Trainer Daly

was reported to have suggested to Feustel that the two colts be kept apart, it being implied over the years that the Jeffordses' trainer was intimating that he was offering Feustel a favor. As one might suspect even from this distance, anyone connected to Man o' War's first six races would have developed a bit of confidence. Out of the offer came not an agreed armistice, but an extra combat, another private trial between the two aces. Johnny Loftus did not habitually include morning races on his schedule, so for the three-furlong race another star rider, Carroll Schilling, rode Man o' War. The Riddle colt burst off in front, turned in three consecutive eleven-second furlongs and won by a length. So much for the suggestion which Golden Broom's earlier trials had engendered. It should be credited to Walter Jeffords and trainer Daly, however, that they were game to put their star in against Man o' War, at equal weight of 130 pounds, in the Sanford. Golden Broom entered that race off a fine victory in the Saratoga Special. Also in the field was Upset, back to try again with a fifteen-pound pull in weights.

In the immediacy of reporting upon what he had just seen, a *New York Times* reporter filed a piece that made mention of Man o' War's misfortune, but praised both the colt and Loftus for their efforts. The piece was published on August 14, without a byline: "The Glen Riddle Farm's great two-year-old, Man o' War... met with his first defeat here today in the running of the Sanford Memorial...Though defeated, Man o' War was not discredited. On the contrary, the manner in which he ran his race stamped him, in the opinion of horsemen, as the best of his division without doubt... There was scarcely a witness of this race who did not believe after it was all over that Man o' War would have walked home with anything like a fair chance." [2]

At the time of the Sanford, the regular starter, Mars Cassidy, was ill, and C. H. Pettingill was called in to take his place. Pettingill was an experienced former starter who was then a placing judge, but he was along in years. He was presumably twenty-six seasons past the low point in his professional career, that having occurred when it took him one and a half hours to get the field away for the 1893 American Derby. Ahead, however, lurked an even darker blot — justified or not.

Golden Broom had seen his status as Man o' War's equal shattered, but he certainly was to have a part to

play in bringing down the great horse's colors. First, prior to the start, Golden Broom broke through the barrier prematurely three times. The resulting hub-bub and milling about may well have had its effect on Pettingill, who, according to the *Times* report, "spent several minutes trying to get the horses lined up and then sent them away with only those near the rail ready for the start." Man o' War was drawn next to the outside and got away poorly, but two of the field were away even worse. Almost certainly, he would not have been actually facing completely the opposite direction at the moment of the start, but horror stories of his facing "the wrong way" may well have meant he was turned sideways, or approximately so. In seven races that day, the *Times* opined, old Charlie Pettingill orchestrated only two clean starts.

The official *Daily Racing Form* chart described the start as "poor and slow," but it should be taken into account that the prevailing description then employed for a good start was the seemingly contradictory phrase "good and slow." The *Times* and the chart reported that Golden Broom, with Eddie Ambrose aboard, took the early lead and that Upset, ridden by Willie Knapp, was closest in pursuit. Loftus, attempting to ameliorate the poor start, steered Man o' War to the inside to avoid losing ground on the turn, and he was making up the deficit quickly enough to be fourth after a quarter mile, according to the chart.

Golden Broom seemed in control into the stretch, but suddenly weakened and Upset sailed past. Loftus was in tight quarters along the rail and, despairing of finding room, veered Man o' War outside, where-upon he charged at Upset but failed to overcome the Whitney colt's advantage. According to the imperfect science of chart calling, Man o' War was no more than two lengths behind after a quarter-mile (:23 1/5) and about the same distance off the pace after a half-mile (:46 4/5). He lost by a half-length as Upset won in 1:11 1/5, only four-fifths of a second over the track record. The *Times* report continued:

"...Man o' War received a fine ride from Loftus, who gave the colt every assistance within his power. Steadily, Man o' War drew up on Upset. A hundred feet from the wire he was three-fourths of a length away. At the wire, he was a scant neck out of first position."

The chart caller, true to his craft, contented himself

with "responding gamely to punishment, (Man o' War) was gaining in the closing strides." He called the margin a half-length.

In *The Great Ones*, Kent Hollingsworth quoted another "contemporary account" that waxed more emotional, and critical: "Man o' War is the champion. He never was so great as he was in defeat…He overcame two of his rider's errors and would have made amends for the third if it had not been committed so close to the winning post. He stood a drive such as no other colt has been asked to do in the last twenty years without flinching…Never again will his courage be questioned henceforth. It was an unknown quality, for he had never before been put to test. When the test came, he was not found wanting…" Hervey identified as the source of this comment the "Metropolitan reviewer" W. C. Vreeland.

Perhaps such observations put into motion the rampant second-guessing which fueled the desire to find blame. Historian Edward Hotaling found *The New York Times* soon doing an about face. Despite the earlier praise of Loftus, by September 7 the paper was railing that "It was the fault of Loftus and not Man o' War that caused the colt to be left at the post," and, further that, the colt still would have won "...but for a bungling ride in which Loftus found every pocket on the track." [3] Later, even John Hervey seemed to concur, stating that Loftus tried to get through on the rail or between horses three times before, at length, swinging to the outside.

Years later, Upset's rider, Willie Knapp, seemed to put down the result to one instant (aside possibly from the start). Knapp was quoted in a lengthy description emanating from Gulfstream Park:

"...Man o' War didn't make his bid till we hit the turn, and then he churned up along the rail till his head bobbed into the corner of my eye. There he was tossin' those twenty-eight foot (sic) strides of his and tryin' to squeeze through on the inside of Golden Broom and Upset. If I'd given so much as an inch, the race would've been as good as over, but jockeys don't ride that way. I could have breezed past Golden Broom any time I took my feet out of the dashboard, but that would also have let Man o' War out of his mouse trap and he'd have whooshed past us in half a dozen strides. When Johnny Loftus saw we weren't going to

open up, there was nothing left for him but to pull up sharply and duck to the outside. That's what I'd been waiting for. That same moment I gunned Upset with my bat…Man o' War then had to come out around and it cost him all of two lengths…he was chargin' like a jet plane, but Upset had just enough left to push his head down in front.

"Sure, I win the race all right — it was the biggest thrill o' my life — but lookin' back at it now there's sure one horse which should of retired undefeated… If I'd moved over just an eyelash that day at Saratoga, he'd have beat me from here to Jaloppy.

"Sometimes I'm sorry I didn't do it."

That the contemporary consensus saw the Sanford as a fluke was eloquently stated by the public ten days later. Again going six furlongs in the Grand Union Hotel Stakes, Man o' War under 130 pounds was 11-20. Upset this time was getting only five pounds. Golden Broom, who had begun to suffer from a quarter crack and never won another race, was not in the field.

There must have been some, however, who at least wanted to believe that the Sanford uncovered a vulner- ability in Man o' War, for a field of ten went to the post.

The start was delayed for five minutes before the common "good and slow" start. Upset was gunned into the lead in the initial strides, but Man o' War was soon lapped on him and was given a head at the call after a quarter-mile in a blazing :22 3/5. Whether they were twenty-six-foot or twenty-eight-foot strides he was "tossin' at" Knapp and Upset, they scooted him right away to a three-length lead over a half-mile in :46 2/5. In the final strides, Loftus eased up Man o' War, but this time his reaction was not one to be examined for the rest of civilization. Man o' War still had a full length on Upset at the finish, reached in 1:12.

The Hopeful was the remaining two-year-old target at Saratoga, and Man o' War was the 1-5 favorite at the last posting of odds. Again the size of the field seemed to indicate some trainers were in denial, Rowe foremost among them as he sent Upset back out. Man o' War was again carrying 130 pounds and giving five to the Whitney colt. Two new rivals had materialized in the form of the splendid young fillies Cleopatra and Constancy. After the field was at the post for twelve minutes, Constancy rushed off with such speed that she held a two-length lead after a quarter-mile in :23. Man

o' War was second. After a half-mile, Constancy still had a length on the colt, clocking :47. Such fractions over a slow track, and with a superstar breathing down her neck, doomed the filly, and Man o' War cruised by to lead by five in the stretch, before slacking off for a four-length win in 1:13. The final quarter-mile took twenty-six seconds, but was more than sufficient. Cleopatra closed to finish second, four lengths ahead of Constancy.

But one race remained on Man o' War's juvenile schedule. After four races in the month of August, he was off for only two weeks, coming out for the thirtieth running of the climactic Futurity Stakes at Belmont Park on September 13. Nine opposed him, although conditions of the race reduced his weight to 127 pounds after a half-dozen consecutive starts under 130.

Trainer Rowe designated Upset as a Whitney stable martyr one more time, but this time he had another hope in the up-and-coming Whitney homebred, John P. Grier. Upset carried 120, John P. Grier 117. After eight minutes at the start, the break was "good and slow" and Sam Hildreth's Dominique set out to earn his two furlongs of fame. He led after that distance (no fractions were recorded on the straight course). Man o' War, third early, had swooped into a half-length lead after a half-mile and John P. Grier had moved up to second, fighting hard. In the final furlongs, Man o' War drew away to win by two and a half lengths "easing up," according to the chart, which credited runner-up John P. Grier with finishing "gamely through the last eighth." Dominique was third. The time of 1:11 3/5 was three seconds off the straight track record at Belmont for the distance.

That was it. At last, there was time to breathe. Man o' War had won nine of ten and earned $83,325. While it was not yet evident that the Upset upset would remain the only event to deprive him of a perfect record, the lone loss at two already was bemoaned by horsemen who likened him to Colin and regretted he did not match the other's unbeaten status. On the other hand, Rowe was at least one fellow who harbored hope that the next year would find the scales at a different balance.

There was no official handicap in America until The Jockey Club sponsored the Experimental Free Handicap for 1933. However, *Daily Racing Form* handicapper C. C. Ridley published a ranking of two-year-olds of 1919 and placed Man o' War on top at 136

pounds. Blazes, who had been third in the Grand Union Hotel, was second at 120. The sixteen-pound spread bespoke the fact that Man o' War already had earned a widespread reverence.

Already, Man o' War was a national sporting figure. Hervey recalled that "...it was from his victory in the Hopeful Stakes onward that the career of Man o' War began to be followed by a largesse of praise that soon became unprecedented...Publications of all kinds, in which ordinarily no notice whatsoever was paid to such an animal as a race horse, featured him conspicuously...Editors made it a policy to headline him, knowing that by doing so they were sure to please their readers. As for the cameramen, could they have had their way, he would have had no rest. They haunted his footsteps, on and off the race course. He was dubbed 'the most photographed horse in the world' and that he deserved the title is beyond contradiction."

MAN o' WAR

CHAPTER 4

What A Marvel

A magnificent two-year-old is a magnificent two-year-old for one of two reasons: Either he is extraordinarily precocious, virtually as developed at two as he ever will be, or he is blessed with such exceptional qualities that he dominates even though he, like his contemporaries, is a stripling with considerable development still to come. The first kind, like a junior high football player with a full beard, will "come back" to his contemporaries and may not remain at the top of the lot at three. The second type has the scope to develop into a superb three-year-old and older horse, and is the sort likely to be recalled as a "great" horse in succeeding years.

If rival owners and trainers hoped that Man o' War had reached his individual peak in his two-year-old form, they would not have been encouraged to see what Feustel was seeing back at Berlin, Maryland, in the autumn and winter of 1919-1920. Despite the chasm between Man o' War and his fellow juveniles, Feustel would recall that he had never seen a horse come forward as much from two to three as Man o' War. The recorded facts bore out his awe: At Saratoga, Man o' War had weighed 970 pounds. Over the winter, he filled out to 1,150, and his height reached 16.2 hands.

He was already a public hero and, now with the War behind America and a era of bustling maturation awaiting the nation, sports figures such as Babe Ruth, Red Grange, and Jack Dempsey were ready to create a distinctive spice for a decade to be known as the "Roaring Twenties." (Prohibition had a role in that flavor, too.) Setting aside for the moment that "roaring" is a term used for a wind deficiency in racehorses, no sports figure was to "roar" louder in a positive sense than Man o' War in this engulfing Golden Age.

Sam Riddle was heading into the second of the racing seasons that were changing his life and assigning him an identity forever viewed as an entry with Man o' War. Horses, however, had always been a part of the identity of this sportsman whom J. K. M. Ross had likened to a British general. Riddle was born on July 1, 1861, in Glen Riddle, Pennsylvania, a village named for his father, who had established a textile plant. The land had been settled by a grandfather, and the name Glen Riddle paid tribute to the Scotch-Irish ancestry on the male side of the Riddles. On his mother's side, Sam Riddle was of Quaker stock. Riddle's father also had been associated with the Whitney-Widener-Elkins syndicate which had created the railways in Philadelphia and New York; thus, there was a distant, ironic link to the career of Man o' War's breeder, August Belmont II.

Sam Riddle participated in the family firm, but was essentially an outdoorsman. He told the story that as a virtual infant he had been lifted onto a horse "some time during the War Between the States," and by the time he reached manhood, he had chivvied many a fox across the bucolic countryside of Pennsylvania's hunt country.

Riddle was president of Pennsylvania's Rose Tree Hunt, said to be the oldest such organization in America, and he established Mr. Riddle's Hounds. He also rode with the Radnor Hunt. Riddle married the former Elizabeth Dobson, whose family also had major textile holdings and who was said to be one

Man o' War as a young
horse — as a suck-
ling (above), yearling
(right), and two-year-
old (below, pictured
with, starting third
from left, John Loftus,
Samuel Riddle, and
Louis Feustel)

August Belmont II (below), breeder of Man o' War. Clocking works with Louis Feustel in 1924 (right); Talking with trainer Sam Hildreth (on right) in 1914 at Belmont Park (bottom right).

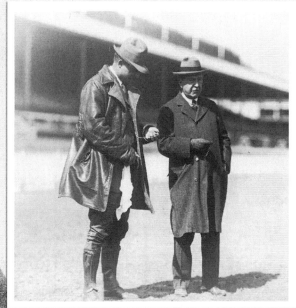

Samuel D. Riddle (below); with his wife, Elizabeth Riddle (left); and with Big Red himself (bottom).

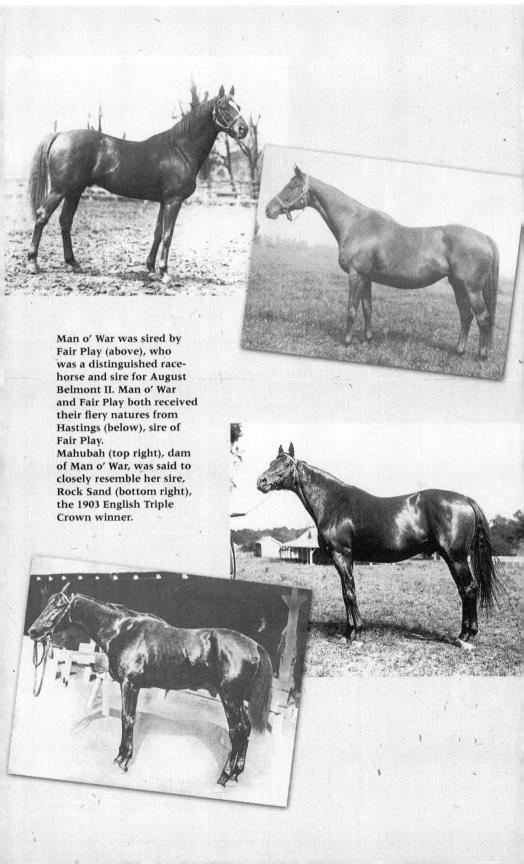

Man o' War was sired by
Fair Play (above), who
was a distinguished race-
horse and sire for August
Belmont II. Man o' War
and Fair Play both received
their fiery natures from
Hastings (below), sire of
Fair Play.
Mahubah (top right), dam
of Man o' War, was said to
closely resemble her sire,
Rock Sand (bottom right),
the 1903 English Triple
Crown winner.

Man o' War knew
defeat only once —
in the 1919 Sanford
Stakes when he lost
to Upset (above).
Jockey John Loftus
(left), Man o' War's
regular rider, was
denied a riding
license over suspi-
cions about the loss.

Man o' War going to the post for the 1919 Belmont Futurity (top, No. 1), and after winning the race by two and a half lengths "easing up" (above). The Futurity was Man o' War's final start at two.

Jockey Clarence Kummer (right) became Man o' War's regular rider during the colt's three-year-old season.

With victories in the Preakness and Belmont Stakes (top) to his credit, Man o' War became "The World's Champion Race Horse" (bottom) at three.

Mr. Riddle

Man O' War
The World's Champion Race Horse

Man o' War faced a true challenge in the stretch of the 1920 Dwyer Stakes from John P. Grier (#2, above). The two met again in the Travers Stakes (top), but Man o' War won "under restraint" by two and a half lengths. In his career finale, Man o' War met 1919 Triple Crown winner Sir Barton in a match race at Kenilworth Park (top, facing page). Man o' War led throughout to win easily.

Man o' War made a farewell tour on his way to Kentucky and never failed to attract admirers, including well-known evangelist Billy Sunday (above). Man o' War (with groom John Buckner, below) first stood at Hinata Farm before moving to Riddle's Faraway Farm.

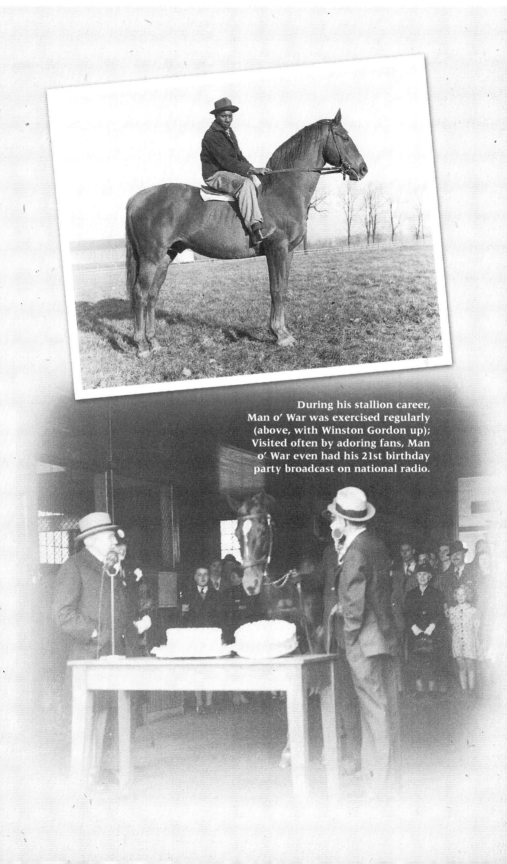

During his stallion career, Man o' War was exercised regularly (above, with Winston Gordon up); Visited often by adoring fans, Man o' War even had his 21st birthday party broadcast on national radio.

"Big Red" and his beloved groom, Will Harbut, are pictured in April of 1947 (above, below). Both died later that year, Man o' War on November 1 and Harbut less than a month before.

Man o' War's best offspring included 1937 Triple Crown winner War Admiral (top, right); 1941 Massachusetts Handicap winner War Relic (below); 1929 Kentucky Derby winner Clyde Van Dusen (below, right); and three-time Maryland Hunt Cup winner Blockade (bottom).

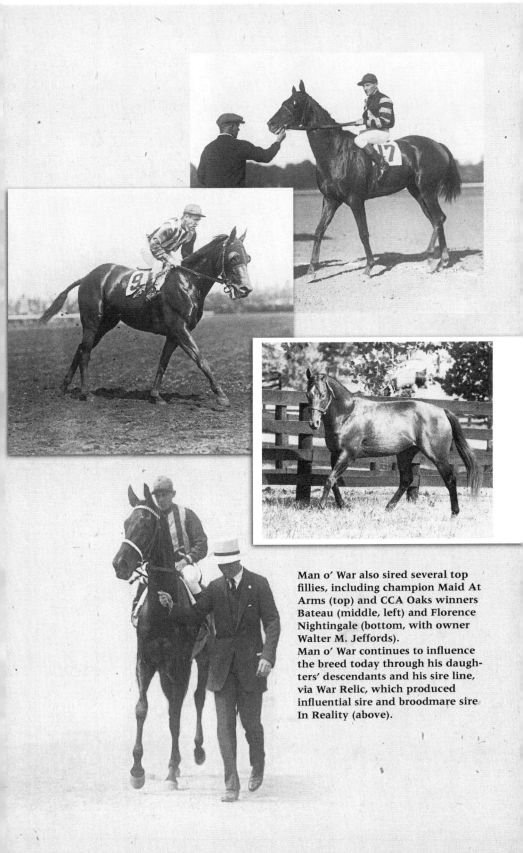

Man o' War also sired several top fillies, including champion Maid At Arms (top) and CCA Oaks winners Bateau (middle, left) and Florence Nightingale (bottom, with owner Walter M. Jeffords).

Man o' War continues to influence the breed today through his daughters' descendants and his sire line, via War Relic, which produced influential sire and broodmare sire In Reality (above).

The barn (above) and farm sign (right) at Faraway Farm, where Man o' War stood for most of his stud career. Man o' War resided in the front left stall. Man o' War was buried at Faraway Farm, and his statue later was placed over the grave. A reported 500 people attended the funeral, which was broadcast on radio. Lexington broadcaster Ted Grizzard gave listeners a step-by-step account of the casket being lowered into the grave.

Man o' War was buried entire in a massive, lined casket. The statue of the great horse was unveiled in 1948. Sculpted by Herbert Haseltine, the statue and Man o' War's remains later were transferred to the Kentucky Horse Park.

of the wealthier women of her era. The 6,000-acre Riddle farm in Pennsylvania raised Hereford, Guernsey, Jersey, and Ayrshire cattle, as well as poultry and hogs. In addition, the Riddles had a 17,000-acre farm on the Eastern Shore of Maryland. As a sportsman, Riddle enjoyed a varied menu, including raccoon hunting on the Maryland estate. He was quoted as describing the activity as requiring "a lamp, two hounds, and a quart." Of course, the quarry was a needed element, as well, but one presumes Riddle relied on nature and did not have to develop a pack of "Mr. Riddle's Raccoons."

Insofar as equine sport was concerned, Riddle was not only a foxhunter and owner but a success-ful trainer of show horses before turning to racing. He had been educated at Dr. John Ferris' Classical Academy and then at Pennsylvania Military College and Swarthmore College. [1] At Swarthmore, he became friends with John Howard Lewis, who was to become known as the greatest steeplechase trainer of his time. Owners Lewis trained for in subsequent years included P. A. B. Widener II's father, Joseph E. Widener, also of the Philadelphia scene. Riddle had steeplechasers be-fore owning flat runners. His first important horse for flat racing was named for the alma mater. Lewis had bred the horse named Swarthmore from a mare he had purchased from President Ulysses S. Grant.

Swarthmore was owned by Riddle and Lewis, but for some reason they had the artist Henry Stull race the horse in his name. Swarthmore won the Kenner Stakes in 1887. During the 1890s, Riddle raced some horses at the old Gloucester track in New Jersey. His Passmore and Sea Bird were said to have been "useful" runners.

It was not until Yankee Witch that Riddle employed the silks of black, yellow sash, yellow hoops on sleeves, that would be flown by Man o' War, War Admiral, and others. Yankee Witch was purchased at two in 1916 from John E. Madden, and she won the Rosedale and Spinaway Stakes for Riddle.

Among Riddle's firmly held opinions about horse racing was that one and one-quarter miles in May was too stern a test for a three-year-old. Thus, although the Kentucky Derby had taken on increased national status since Harry Payne Whitney's Regret won it in 1915, Riddle did not allow Feustel to prepare Man o' War for that event. (It was not until War Admiral in 1937 that Riddle relented, the Derby having taken on even more

importance by that time because of the rising glamour of the Triple Crown.)

Man o' War's first target at three, then, was the Preakness Stakes. The Preakness had been run first at Pimlico in 1873, but had seemingly disappeared for some years early in the century. It was revived at Pimlico in 1909 and was run in two divisions in 1918. Thus, the chart of Man o' War's running was designated as the "thirteenth," it apparently being someone's interpretation that the modern Preakness dated only from the revival. Eventually, research revealed that a race named the Preakness had been contested in New York during those blank years, so today, the history of the Preakness has been righted to include all runnings back to 1873.

Nevertheless, the Preakness in 1920 was sufficiently important to Marylanders that Stuart Janney Jr. recalled having missed school to see the three-year-old debut of the great Man o' War. (Years later, Janney and his wife would contribute their own version of greatness as breeders and owners of the flying black filly Ruffian.)

The Preakness, then one and one-eighth miles, was

run on May 18, slightly more than eight months since Man o' War's last start at two. The horse was 4-5, even though he had had no prep race and would be facing, who else, but Upset. Rowe had prepared Whitney's colt a bit earlier, and he had run a strong race in the Kentucky Derby ten days earlier, losing by a head to Paul Jones. On Watch, Donnacona, and Blazes also had been prominent in the Derby field, underscoring the quality of competition Man o' War had treated with such disdain at two.

Riddle was quoted by Hervey that "it was a terribly hot day, the crowd was enormous, and our stable so situated that it was necessary for Man o' War to thread his way through a mass of motor cars in order to get to the saddling paddock. The only way in which we got him there in safety was through the aid of the police, who had to clear a path for him. This was the only time I ever saw him much upset before he went into a race."

(Man o' War bolted during the parade, but relieved his helpless rider by coming to a stop fairly soon.)

A field of nine contested the Preakness, and under the allowance conditions of the race at that time, the weights varied from Man o' War's 126 pounds down

to 114. Upset was in at 122, Blazes also 126. The field was at the post for six minutes before the usual, "good and slow" start. Man o' War was ridden for the first time in a race by Clarence Kummer, who had worked him some in the mornings late in his two-year-old season. (Loftus did not ride after 1919, a subject to be addressed later.) Man o' War rushed into the lead heading into the first turn and set a swift pace. He had a daylight margin over King Thrush (114) after a quarter-mile. He had stretched the margin to four lengths after six furlongs and then had no trouble holding off Upset, who came on to be second. The final margin was one and a half lengths, which fit within a range of margins Man o' War would employ several times that year — not spectacular, but more dignified than letting a horse actually finish lapped beside his majestic presence. Upset was five lengths clear of third place Wildair. The times were :23 2/5, :47 3/5, 1:12 2/5, 1:38 1/5, and 1:51 3/5. He missed the track record by only three-fifths of a second.

Kummer, who had ridden Sir Barton and Exterminator, immediately anointed Man o' War "the greatest one I have ever ridden."

Riddle was said to be "badly mussed" by the time he emerged from the crowd, who took the attitude that Man o' War was a "Marylander." This must have been uncomfortable for the stylish gentleman.

There was more bad news for Man o' War's rivals, although they could not know it yet. In the eleven days before his next race, Feustel later recalled, Man o' War "improved more than any horse I ever knew in so short a space." Without knowledge of this, other trainers were already backing off. The Withers brought out only a field of three (a fourth was scratched), despite Man o' War having been left out of the original entries and added later under rules then prevailing. It was the first of eight consecutive races in which Man o' War would have only one or two horses face him. The Withers called for all starters to carry 118 pounds, a trifling package to Man o' War.

Hervey quoted one unnamed observer's waxing eloquent: "...those who had seen racing in every part of the world were ready to place him on the topmost pinnacle of the hippic temple of fame."

The great horseman John E. Madden added his own testimony: "What struck me...was the spirit of

the immense crowd. It rose to Man o' War with won-derful enthusiasm (although) the odds were prohibi-tive and I do not think there was $1,000 bet on him."

If competition could not force Man o' War to come close to his best, the lust for speed within the horse himself was sufficient. The Withers marked the first record for the great colt. He again led from the start, always had Wildair measured by at least a couple of lengths, and won by two. Wildair, yet another Whitney horse with whom Rowe sought to lower Man o' War's colors, was twelve lengths clear of the remaining runner, David Harum. The fractions of the one-mile race were :24, :47 1/5, 1:11, and the final time of 1:35 4/5 beat the old Belmont Park mark by nearly a second. Moreover, it was a new American record, reducing the old mark held by Fairy Wand by two-fifths of a second.

That was the first of eight times that year that Man o' War would set or equal track or American records, and the distances of those records marched upward: one mile, one and one-sixteenth miles, one and one-eighth, one and one-quarter, one and three-eighths, one and one-half, and one and five-eighths miles.

The Belmont Stakes on June 12 has been long revered as a test of a champion. For Man o' War and Kummer, it was a pleasant ride in the park in a two-horse town. G. W. Loft, the owner of Donnacona, stepped forward to accept the $1,500 second money in the so-called $10,000-guaranteed event. Not even James Rowe had a starter for this one. Man o' War led all the way and could not be restrained to make it a normal margin. He drew farther away with virtually every furlong and beat his lonely foe by twenty lengths. There were no fractions recorded, but the final time of 2:14 1/5 set a new American record for one and three-eighth miles, then the classic's distance. The mark bettered by more than three seconds the record set only the previous year by the first Triple Crown winner, Sir Barton. The latter was still in training, and a meeting of the two colts was an obvious event racing men yearned to see. (The Belmont was described in the chart as having a "guaranteed value" of $10,000. Apparently, the guarantee did not apply to a two-horse field, for Man o' War won a purse of $7,700.

Ten days after the Belmont, Feustel dropped Man o' War back to a mile for Jamaica's Stuyvesant Handicap.

The weight was a staggering 135, but again only one horse showed up to give it a go. This was Yellow Hand, in at 103 pounds. The gulf in weights was unequal to the gulf in class, for Man o' War established a five-length lead after a quarter-mile and won by eight. The times of :25 3/5, :49, 1:14 1/5, and 1:41 3/5 reflected the slowing conditions of the track and lack of urgency.

Nearly three weeks later, Man o' War again won a two-horse race, but this was a considerably different affair. Through the years, the Dwyer has enjoyed the aura of "the only time a horse ever went with him" even though Man o' War had been led through the initial stages of other races. However, the Dwyer marked the only time a horse went with Man o' War AND was still there to be nagging him in the stretch. All in all, the Dwyer probably was the truest test for courage to which Man o' War was ever subjected.

Odd is this concept of courage: We tend to revere it in horses to the extent that it sometimes overshadows pure speed and brilliance. One of the owners of Seattle Slew has confided how tiresome it is to hear so much about Slew's barely failing to retake Exceller in the Jockey Club Gold Cup. Should not his many victories

— take, for example winning the Triple Crown while still unbeaten — take precedence in people's memory? But, we say, he generally was so superior that he rarely was tested for courage; in the Gold Cup he was severely tested, and showed plenty of it. Similarly, as we have seen, Man o' War himself received the most resounding of praise for gallantry as a result of his singular defeat! Odd, indeed.

Of course, it had to be James Rowe who had the bit in his teeth again. The fellow who had trained unbeaten Colin, had won a New York Handicap Triple Crown with Whisk Broom II, and had even won the Kentucky Derby with a filly (Regret), had not been among those who took Man o' War to his heart. No doubt he recognized the qualities of the colt, but every galloping triumph, every headline, every track record, must have been a tweaking of the sore tooth to Rowe.

Rowe had tried Man o' War seven times and was one and six — the one in the Sanford festooned with so many emotional asterisks as virtually to obscure it. Now, he had Futurity runner-up John P. Grier at the top of his form, off two victories at three, and he had not been reserved in announcing that the Dwyer

Stakes, one and one-eighth miles at Aqueduct on July 10, would be his target. Rowe must have salivated over the allowance conditions, which — taking into account his horse's earnings and record vis-a-vis the splendid recent wins of Man o' War — dictated that his colt would carry only 108 pounds, to Man o' War's 126!

Kummer, however, had ridden both colts, and said, while Grier was "marvelously fast," he could not beat Man o' War.

The New York Times' Fred Van Ness, who had reported on the Sanford, was back at it and in splendid form himself:

"Man o' War had been referred to as the champion throughout this season, but all the while there was one colt which he had not met...John P. Grier was the last of the good ones of his age to be sent after the mighty son of Fair Play...It was a smashing race viewed from any angle. It was a struggle between two really great horses...those in the stands...saw Man o' War forced to run his very best, his rider obliged to go to the whip in the stretch drive after the contestants had set such a dazzling pace from the very start that they seemed fairly to fly through space rather than touch ground."

Walter Vosburgh [2] quoted Riddle as more or less micro-managing the scenario when Kummer asked "how shall I ride?" (Did jockeys in 1920 really talk that way?) "Lay along with Grier all the way, and if you find you can win, don't try to ride him out, but win by a length or two lengths," Riddle allegedly said. "Mr. Feustel tells me Man o' War 'isn't screwed up right tight,' and I don't want more use made of him than is necessary to win." (Riddle must have forgotten to request that Kummer have the winner's ears pricked for effect at the finish, for the commonly published photo of the finish finds Man o' War with one ear cocked, the other back.)

As matters transpired, the two colts "lay along" with each other from the start. The track at that time was one and one-quarter miles, so that a one and one-eighth-mile race started from a chute which joined the backstretch. The larger Man o' War broke on the inside, and so evenly matched were they early on that some writers reported a fleeting impression that Grier had been left. He was invisible to the crowd for the best of reasons, i.e., he was running stride for stride with a Colossus.

Eddie Ambrose on John P. Grier kept the Whitney

colt right at Man o' War's throatlatch through most of the race. The pace, as Van Ness suggested, was astounding. They went the first quarter-mile in :23 2/5, Man o' War in front by a half-length briefly. Then they stepped it up. After a second quarter-mile in :22 3/5 (half-mile, :46), Grier was again virtually nose to nose. They slowed ever so slightly for a third quarter in :23 3/5 (six furlongs, 1:09 3/5). There was a minute dispute with this *Daily Racing Form* chart fraction; Van Ness said the six-furlong clocking was one-fifth faster and thus was better than the American record for the distance.

Still, Grier clung to Man o' War. Their early efforts, and the laws of nature, dictated a cessation of this madness. The next quarter-mile required :26 2/5. Man o' War had taken John P. Grier's best punch and was still standing, but so was Grier! Incredibly, the crowd of more than 25,000 could go home and say they attended a race in which Man o' War saw his lead disappear in the stretch. Grier got his head in front: Rowe must have felt the flutter of vindication rising in his thorax. Kummer did something rarely needed: He reached back with his whip and brought it down upon Man o' War's flank. Once at two, the colt had been noted to have responded gamely to "punishment" in racing's overly harsh jargon. Now, he was under the gun again.

Only in the stable had Man o' War theretofore been known as "Big Red," but now his trainer began shouting over and over for all the world to hear, "Come on, Big Red! Come on, Big Red!" — one of the nicknames forever to be assigned the horse. As Feustel told racing writer-official Pat O'Brien years later, he had positioned himself, as was his wont, in the infield between the furlong pole and sixteenth-mile pole, and he had recognized that Grier for a moment had put his head in front! "The jockey gave Red a couple of whacks and he took off. So did I. I started to run down toward the finish line, yelling all the way. Near the finish there was a little ditch in the infield and I was so excited and didn't see it and fell in. You know, I never did see the actual finish of the Dwyer."

What the trainer missed was Man o' War surging ahead, seeming to have it won, but then having to turn back one last effort from the heart and sinews of John P. Grier. Man o' War was challenged, but perhaps unruffled. Even Grier could postpone his own demise

only so long, for in the final fifty yards, he fell away —
weary, and spent but a new name in the honor roll of
courage. Man o' War won by one and one-half lengths.
The final furlong took thirteen and a fifth seconds, but
the composite clocking for the mile and one-eighth
was 1:49 1/5, another new American record.

(A unique gene seemingly common to all horsemen
prompted Feustel years later to have harbored one
more detail for the retelling of the story of the Dwyer:
"One of the things few people know is that Man o' War
broke from a wet, greasy place in the track, where the
water wagon had been standing," he told *Daily Racing
Form*'s Charlie Hatton two score-plus years later.)

Reporter Van Ness was sensitive to the public's love
of — not just respect for — Man o' War: "For just a
second there loomed the possibility of the horse of
the century meeting defeat. It was a rather sickening
thought to those who had raised this colt to a pedes-
tal." He quoted jockey Kummer as saying:

"John P. Grier had his head in front for a moment
at the eighth pole, but the moment I went after him in
earnest the race was over. As to whether Man o' War
was all in, well, when horses run like they did from the

start something has to crack and while I would not like to say how much Man o' War had left, it was enough so that he could have gone on to give another horse a battle had there been a third horse in the race. He ran a hard race, but he was not all in at the end."

The great journalist and racing announcer Clem McCarthy was quoted by Hervey in his staccato style:

"...For one flashing moment — Grier's nose in front!

"He's got h__!"

"We never finished the 'him! ' "

"Once or twice Ambrose fanned Grier's sides, but gently. For Eddie knew many seconds earlier what none of the rest of us could see...Ambrose knew it would be cruel to punish John P. Grier..."

Man o' War's glory was now at its height, and the stunning thing about him was that it never would be diminished. For all the visceral impact he had on those who saw him, however, he was not hailed as a "perfect" specimen by those who evaluate the physical conformation of a racehorse against the presumed ideal of form for function.

"Man o' War was a red chestnut, marked with a star and an indistinct short gray stripe in his forehead.

He had a straight profile, large nostrils, stout neck, and was rather broad across the chest — more so than we like to see," wrote Walter Vosburgh, for many years a distinguished racing official as well as historian. "His back was rather longer than the average, and he 'cut away' slightly behind the croup. His legs were straight, and his pasterns none too long. His feet were of fair size. He had the size and power of a sprinter, with the conformation of a stayer."

"He was a trifle coarse, his head too high, and his forelegs forked a bit wide," J. A. Estes recalled. Even trainer Feustel, who must have idolized the horse, was quoted that, "He was always a big, long, lean thing in training, nothing like so smooth and full of quality (refinement) as his sire Fair Play."

As for coat color, Man o' War's, like many chestnuts, was particularly changeable in appearance according to sunlight. We recall Hewitt describing his as "copper colored" when seen in the shade of the Belmont Park paddock. Estes wrote years later of the question over whether his coat would be best described in terms of reds or golds.

In addition to glorious triumphs, of course, a great

horse brings tensions, worries, sometimes clashes of egos. At the height of his fame, the down side of owning and training Man o' War included threats of a physical nature, some vague, others specific. There were times when Riddle and Feustel were warned that "something is going to happen," which set off all manner of concerns ranging from the horse being injured to drugged for some nefarious betting coup. Someone always slept in the barn, only feet away from the horse.

One bizarre incident took place soon after the horse's retirement when Harry T. Lamey was arrested on charges of having sent letters threatening to kill Man o' War and Mrs. Riddle unless he was paid $10,000. It reportedly turned out that three years earlier, Lamey had been assigned to make an estimate for wiring the Riddle farm for electricity and the idea of illegally tapping into the family wealth was born. The advent of Man o' War gave him an additional venue.

Even well-meaning, adoring fans could be a threat, as Riddle noted, and policemen on various occasions had to protect Man o' War from members of his public who thought plucking hairs from his mane or tail a

perfectly okay method of souvenir hunting. Fears of a horse being admired so adamantly that he is beaten by his own fame are not far-fetched: Fairway was so harried by mane- and tail-hair souvenir hunters as he made his way toward the start of the 1928 Epsom Derby that he came apart and was badly beaten, while the whirl of popping flash bulbs in the paddock at Longchamp perhaps contributed to the unbeaten Nijinsky II's stunning loss in the 1970 Prix de l'Arc de Triomphe.

Also hovering above the Man o' War camp was an unhappy circumstance involving the colt's jockey at two, Johnny Loftus. So sensational did the defeat of Man o' War in the Sanford Memorial seem afterward that hints of a fix were inevitable. Loftus was one of America's great riders, had scored in all three Triple Crown races on Sir Barton earlier that year, and was the season's leading money-winning jockey, so he would seem a poor candidate for a bribe — especially aboard a great horse. Nevertheless, the fact that both Loftus and Upset's rider, Willie Knapp, were denied licenses for the next year by The Jockey Club — along with that body's penchant in that era for terse, unexplained rulings — guaranteed that suspicion could never be totally erased. (Loftus, who died in 1976, apparently never got over feeling bitter that his glorious year of years was virtually forgotten and the one loss would hound his identity for the rest of his days.)

There was almost certainly no fiber of Sam Riddle that suspected anything foul by Loftus. Riddle went to one meeting of The Jockey Club stewards to appeal to them to reinstate the rider, the reasons for his and Knapp's denial never having been made public. It must have been an uncomfortable moment for Riddle to stand before August Belmont II, hat in hand, so to speak. The two men connected forever in history by Man o' War — both more or less conditioned since birth to having their own way — faced each other, this time one as advocate, the other as supreme judge. Minutes of the meeting merely state that Belmont informed Riddle that the matter could not be reopened. Good-bye, Sam; good-bye Johnny.

The details of the cases of Loftus and Knapp presumably were buried with the only parties that knew all the facts, and, of course, there is no certainty that even those parties were in agreement.

To Riddle, the sting of The Jockey Club stance on

the Loftus matter must have been irritated further by Belmont's tendency to act as if he still had some proprietary interest in the great horse. Abe Hewitt used to be amused by retelling that Belmont so frequently supplied Riddle with advice on how to train and when to run Man o' War that Sam at length turned to Mrs. Belmont to plead, "Eleanor, you've got to make Augie stop talking to me like this. I simply can't stand it."(Neither of the prickly issues dissuaded Riddle from hailing Belmont as "the grandest man of the American Turf" on a much later occasion.)

Further underscoring Riddle's belief in Loftus was his declaration in an interview with Oliver DeWolf twenty years later that "I had the best horse and the best jockey in the world in Man o' War and Loftus."

Relationships with trainer Feustel perhaps were not so cozy. In 1963, Feustel, thinking back to the matter of his not having entered Man o' War initially for the Withers Stakes, told *Daily Racing Form* columnist Charlie Hatton that this was the only occasion when Riddle gave the trainer any flak about handling the horse: "He found fault once. That was when I didn't name him for the Withers when the regular entries closed."

This apparently was a glossing over of memory, purposefully or not. There is reason to suspect that, as the 1920 season went on and the pressure of fame built, there was more than a little friction between owner and trainer. In 1970, in an unattributed obituary of Feustel, *The Blood-Horse* reported that "Feustel quit Riddle several times when Man o' War was racing, and did so permanently in 1921..." but did not elaborate. In her 1997 Eclipse Award-winning article on Man o' War, Maryjean Wall of the *Lexington Herald-Leader* stated as fact that Riddle "grew so paranoid that he hired a private detective to stalk the horse's trainer." [3] More recently, after diligently preparing material for a movie on Man o' War for STEALTH Productions, producer Vicky Fleming told the author that the Pinkerton detective company confirmed that it had once had some files on the horse and trainer, but that the files no longer existed. Again, perhaps a tale never to be explained in full.

Riddle himself might have provided some clue as to what he had been like to work for when he was quoted by DeWolf in 1940 that, "I'm growing old, and you know I've decided to be nice to everyone. I wasn't always."

Through all this, of course, the horse was thriving. The Dwyer win over John P. Grier would come to be known as the final true challenge, but this was not the same as being the final true test. Rowe was not finished, for one thing, and for another the handicapper (assigner of weights) was lurking. The horse would carry as much as 138 pounds before the year was out.

Man o' War had a break of nearly a month after the Dwyer and next started on August 7. The upscale carnival known as Saratoga was having its annual celebration, and Man o' War took up 131 pounds for the one and three-sixteenth-mile Miller Stakes. He opened at 1-30 against a field involving only his old rival Donnacona (119) and a 150-1 shot named King Albert (114). Jockey Kummer had been reminded harshly of the vagaries of life. The Monday after the wondrous Dwyer, the filly Costly Colors had gone down with him. This event proved more "costly" than "colorful," for Kummer suffered a shoulder fracture that kept him out of action for seven weeks. This circumstance created an occasion for perhaps the most noted jockey of the era to ride the most famous horse. He was Earl Sande, and he had no problem with sending Man o' War to the front and touring with a clear, but modest, lead into the stretch, where they drew off to win by six lengths. Donnacona was second, four lengths before King Albert. The clocking sequence was :24, :48 1/5, 1:12 4/5, 1:37 4/5, and 1:56 3/5.

Like Kummer, Sande was awestruck: "I never felt anything under me like that colt in my life. Why, he is a regular machine! He strides farther than anything I ever rode and does it so handily you wouldn't think he was running at all. He is the greatest horse I have ever ridden."

Highlight for three-year-olds during the Saratoga season has traditionally been the one and one-quarter-mile Travers Stakes. Man o' War was sent for it on August 21, two weeks after the Miller. This time, yet another rider, Andy Schuttinger, enjoyed the opportunity to ride the horse of a lifetime.

Kummer had arrived at Saratoga, but a couple of rides left him so sore it was obvious he was not yet fit. Sande had presumed the ride was no longer available and had gone to Windsor, Ontario, for an important race. Among available riders, Riddle chose Schuttinger.

Misgivings of other origins swirled through Sam

Riddle's head. As he later was quoted by Hervey:

"I will own that this was the only time I was ever nervous, really nervous, about the outcome of a race after he had showed us what he was. It was not so much that I had any doubt of his ability to win. Of that I was entirely confident. But I knew he had the two best three-year-olds in America to beat, that is, the two best aside from himself...I knew it was to be two-pluck-one, that Grier had to carry us just as far as he could and then Upset was to come along and finish the killing, if possible.

"I knew that...a lot of people who passed for very smart were backing the Whitney pair down to the shortest odds laid against anything that had started against Man o' War since the Preakness...But over and above that, what had worked me up to a very tense nervous state was the fact that people kept coming to me and warning me that 'something was going to happen' and for me to 'look out for it.' I knew of course that I had nothing to fear from Mr. Whitney or from Jimmy Rowe except the speed and gameness of their entries. But what might come from an outside quarter — that I couldn't tell. So, we watched Man o' War night and day, every second of the time, until he was saddled for the race, and never relaxed our vigilance.

"And as for the race itself, I gave Andy these instructions: 'Keep him there and keep him going. Don't let either of them get near you. Just show them up, if anybody thinks they can beat him. That's all, for he will do the rest.' "

There were only two other starters, but, incredibly it was Rowe v. Red yet again. This time, the dogged trainer was sending both Upset and John P. Grier against the great white whale of his nightmares. Man o' War carried 129, Upset 123, and Grier 115. The stage was set for another search of one another's bravery. Like a long-awaited heavyweight title fight that ends before the crowd is settled, however, the Travers quickly unfolded with little resemblance to any anticipated Dwyer II. The hope of having John P. Grier weaken him with early speed, setting it up for Upset, quickly encountered a snag. Man o' War dashed to an early lead and was in front by a length after a quarter-mile in :23 1/5. A second quarter in :23 2/5 (half, :46 3/5) doubled the margin to two lengths over John P. Grier, and Upset was five farther back. Man o' War kept up approximately the same pace, getting the third quarter in :23 2/5. At that

point, Upset was gaining on John P. Grier, all right, but Man o' War had increased his lead to four lengths. The pace inevitably slackened thereafter, but Man o' War continued to dominate, hitting the mile in 1:35 3/5, and finishing in 2:01 4/5, which equaled the track record. He was under restraint at the end, getting home by two and a half lengths as Upset came on to be second, seven lengths over the one-time challenger, John P. Grier.

Ironically, stewards in the stand that day included R. L. Gerry, who had been the underbidder on Man o' War two years earlier! One can but imagine his emotions as Big Red's career had played out.

The Travers now as then is a key race for the division and almost annually brings together at least a sampling of the best of a crop. Through all the intervening years, no horse ever has matched the feat of Man o' War of being in front after six furlongs in a time as swift as 1:10 in the Travers and still winning the race. (The closest approximations occurred in 1976 and 1994, respectively, when Honest Pleasure and then Holy Bull led their Travers after six furlongs in 1:10 2/5 and still were in front at the wire.)

On September 4, Man o' War stepped up to his

longest race, the Lawrence Realization, at one and five-eighth miles. This obviously engendered no hope of finding a chink in his armor just because he was trying something he had never tried before. Were it not for the sporting decision that Hoodwink would enter in the colors of Mrs. Riddle's niece, Mrs. Jeffords, the race would have been a walkover. Even with that second starter, it was closer to a walkover than a contest, but an additional bit of family drama was involved. Overhearing Riddle's instructions to Kummer, who was back aboard, to let Man o' War roll only the final quarter mile, Mrs. Riddle interceded. Hervey recalled that, in response to a public wish to see Man o' War extended, she said to her husband, "Why not let him run all the way. If he can set a new record, let him do it. The public deserves to see him show what he is and not just canter around the course and sprint the last quarter."

Either for sport or domestic tranquility, Riddle relented: "Let him run," he told the rider!

Man o' War established a twenty-length lead in the first two furlongs and improved his position manyfold. At the end, there was probably considerable comment that he "won by a mile," but the chart callers do not

deal in such hyperbole, so the winning margin was estimated as a rounded off to 100 lengths. Man o' War carried 126 pounds, giving ten to Hoodwink. Despite a total lack of pressure to excel, he excelled for the sake of his own spirit, setting a new American record of 2:40 4/5. One can only presume that Mrs. Riddle was smugly pleased.

The time lowered the eleven-year-old record of Fitz Herbert by more than four seconds. While it is true the one and five-eighths-mile distance is not very common, it is remarkable that Man o' War's record still stood forty years later when the great Kelso won the Realization in the identical time.

Breeder Belmont's organization had started a new event, The Jockey Club Stakes, at one and a half miles in 1919 to provide an additional test of stamina, with three-year-olds meeting their elders. The first running had not gone so well, with Purchase winning in a walkover, and with Man o' War on the scene it was hardly likely to be overcrowded in 1920, either. Damask started for Whitney, but it seems likely that the stable was just helping out. There were no other starters. The only odds reported were 1-100 on Man o' War, 80-1 on Damask. Kummer put Man o' War on the lead, and the horse was four lengths clear after two furlongs. He increased the lead gradually and won by fifteen lengths. His fractions were :25, :49 3/5, 1:14 1/5, 1:38 4/5, and 2:03 2/5. His final clocking of 2:28 4/5 set a new American record for one and a half miles, and that mark stayed in the family even when broken, for it was first bettered by Man o' War's son War Admiral.

Feustel and Riddle elected to submit Man o' War to the handicappers one more time, and he was entered in the Potomac Handicap, which at $10,000 was one of his richest races. The Potomac was raced at the old Havre de Grace track in Maryland, near where Man o' War had wintered but where he had never raced. Perhaps wanting some Maryland locals to have another look at Man o' War colored the judgment. Feustel was said to be negative on the idea, for, in addition to confronting a deepish, tiring track, Man o' War was assigned a stunning 138 pounds. Such weights rarely have been carried even by America's stoutest older horses, and here Man o' War at three was taking on that burden going one and one-sixteenth miles. The circumstance brought out a field

of four, modest sounding, but the largest assemblage Man o' War had faced since the Preakness. Rowe was in for one last try, and since his Wildair was getting an even thirty pounds from the champion he might have harbored some hopes. The others were Blazes in at 104 1/2 pounds and Derby winner Paul Jones at 114.

Moreover, there were reports that Man o' War had had a slight filling in a tendon, a hint of something totally absent from his escutcheon, i. e., lameness. Nevertheless, he was held at odds of 15-100.

Feustel said he never could decide which was Man o' War's greatest race, the Dwyer or the Potomac. At Havre de Grace, Man o' War as usual took the lead and had daylight after a quarter-mile, but he did not draw off. Blazes was first to chase him, then Wildair took over the runner-up spot to put in his best effort. The front pair drew fifteen lengths ahead of third-place Blazes, but Wildair could never bring Man o' War to a drive. The chart noted Man o' War "drew away without effort" when Wildair edged up to try to challenge in the stretch and "was easing up at the finish." The final margin was one and a half lengths. He set a track record of 1:44 4/5 after fractions of :23, :47 3/5, 1:11 3/5, and 1:38 1/5.

Although the Triple Crown series of the Kentucky Derby, Preakness, and Belmont Stakes was not the highly focused target in 1919 that it would become, Sir Barton's sweep of the three races, along with the Withers, had prompted praise in the same category Man o' War would the next year. Indeed, "Horse of the Century" was already being used in *The New York Times*. J. K. L. Ross's Sir Barton was not the consistent star that Man o' War was, but he had come back at four and he hit a spectacular peak at Saratoga when he carried 133 pounds to an American-record one and three-sixteenths-mile victory in the Merchants and Citizens Handicap.

A meeting was natural and had been talked about for some time. Both owners were game. As usually happens in such made-to-order extravaganzas, egos and emotions clashed. Various tracks wanted the race, but A. M. Orpen stunned the world by gaining it by offering a $75,000 purse to hold the race at his pedestrian Kenilworth Park in Windsor, Ontario. Among track operators who tried for the event had been the P. T. Barnum of the Turf, Matt Winn, and when an out-of-the-way Canadian track won the prize, there were

plenty of aspersions that Ross as a Canadian had pulled a low one and that Riddle had been secretly promised a share of the gate. Why already-rich men running for one of the richest purses in history needed to be bribed was not explained.

Other controversy surrounded the Sir Barton camp. The colt was known to be somewhat off his best, and the hard track at Windsor figured to sting his tender feet. Then, his trainer, Guy Bedwell, convinced owner Ross that Sande, although an accomplished rider, was feeling the pressure to an extent that, at his still-young age, he should be replaced. A fellow named Frank Keogh thus inherited the ride on Sir Barton.

Less publicized, but later confirmed by Riddle, Man o' War had struck himself in the testing going of Havre de Grace and had a filling in a leg (or ankle). A few days' rest found him sound enough to continue training.

Ross' son was frank in admitting in his book that, even at his best, Sir Barton was not the horse to bring down Man o' War, but held that his father's hero might have fared better if everything had been perfect. Despite Sir Barton's status, Man o' War was 1-20. The race was one and a quarter miles, with Man o' War as a three-year-old in at 120 pounds and the older Sir Barton carrying 126. It was, everyone knew, meant as a match race, but since match races were against local regulations, a horse name Wickford was named at the entry stage, then scratched. Man o' War "bounded" to the front, read the chart, and Keogh was going to the whip inside the first quarter-mile. Man o' War reeled off fractions of :23, :46 2/5, and 1:11 4/5, after which he had a five-length lead. Sir Barton could do nothing to make an impression, and Man o' War and Kummer raced on, getting the mile in 1:37 2/5 and winning by seven lengths in 2:03. The time reduced the track record by more than six seconds.

J. K. M. Ross wrote years later that his father had been fairly stoic throughout the race, but as he watched Man o' War complete the final race of his career, he overheard the older man utter the simple tribute, "What a Marvel!" Sir Barton's owner then rushed to congratulate Riddle, who invited him to his private train car.

Feustel later was said to have found cut marks on the stirrup leathers of Man o' War's saddle, bringing home the reality that such events can generate suf-

ficient greed that nothing can be taken for granted. Fortunately, if indeed, foul play had intended to make sure Kummer fell, it was a botched job. Illustrative of the sums being passed about, it was said that the high-rolling gambler Chicago O'Brien bet $100,000 on Man o' War, despite the cramped odds of 1-20. When it was suggested this was a foolhardy proposition, O'Brien riposted, "Can you tell me any other way I could make $5,000 in two minutes?"

Man o' War had thus completed his three-year-old season the way he began it, in isolated splendor. There had been eleven starts and eleven wins. No trainer can be expected to deliver a horse in perfect pitch for every start, but Feustel's job had been masterfully close. If there were any imperfections, Man o' War glossed over them. He had earned $166,140 at three alone. In two seasons, he had won twenty of twenty-one races, and his purse total of $249,465 was an all-time record.

For all the suspicion that some of his pronounce- ments reflected a certain bravado, the way Riddle was later quoted by Hervey in connection to the owning of a superb champion seems more born of honest amaze- ment than aggrandizement:

"Such a horse ceases to be just private property and becomes in effect public property…Even in the case of so great a horse as Man o' War, there is a difference in degree only. You may know he is pounds better than any other horse in training…but you know that a misstep on the race track, a seemingly insignificant accident in the stable, a bad ship, a cold caught by chance, any one of a thousand trivial things may ruin his career. There are also unprincipled persons that must be guarded against, that will not hesitate at anything dastardly. Some of the most famous horses here and abroad have been their victims.

"That it is not a wonderful thing to own a Man o' War I am not trying to assert, for there is no other feeling in the world to compare with it if one loves a great horse. It gives a thrill that nothing else ever can. It cannot be put into words, because words cannot express it."

Man o' War was returned again to Maryland. Riddle turned down an offer for a $50,000 purse to match him again, against the great and popular old gelding Exterminator, and only briefly pondered suggestions to race him at four in England. [4] Riddle also conferred with Walter Vosburgh to see what weights Man o'

War might be expected to carry at four. Vosburgh gave the foreboding estimate that, if Man o' War came back sound and good at four, he would be induced to place the highest weight on him of his career as a handi-capper, perhaps 145 to 150 pounds! Riddle quickly decided to retire the colt.

The crusades were over, and the rightful king had prevailed.

CHAPTER 5

Keeper of the Legend

"T hat was worth coming halfway around the world to hear," the English Lord said warmly to the elderly black gentleman who had been showing, and talking about, the horse. Lord Halifax, Great Britain's ambassador to the United States, thus was recruited into the throngs who for some sixteen years were mesmerized by the wondrous deeds of Man o' War, as told by one Will Harbut.

Man o' War was at stud in Kentucky from 1921 through the 1943 season, when he was retired from service, but the public had access to him until six months before his death four years later. It was said that perhaps a half-million people came to visit him.

He had been at stud for a decade before Will Harbut came into his life, and his sons and daughters had kept the racing, and general sporting, public well reminded of his prowess. Harbut took over as Man o' War's personal PR man.

Time after time, the old stud groom would show visitors other stallions and then, as tension built, lead out the great animal himself — head high and aloof, his coat fairly bursting into silent fireworks in the sunlight.

Then Harbut would give a spiel that began with the fact that Man o' War had been born just a few miles away at Nursery Stud. From his racing career, the Dwyer was the high point: "...and he looked over to that Whitney horse and he said, `Now you come on, Grier, if you can' ...and a man comes here and offers a million dollars for him and Mr. Riddle says, 'No, lots of men might have a million dollars, but only one man can have Man o' War.' "

These dramatic phrases might be punctuated with a staccato "Stand still Red," and invariably led to something like "he beat all the records and beat all the horses and there wasn't nothin' left for him to do...He was the mostest hoss that ever was."

Just as Riddle was always identified with Man o' War, Harbut and Big Red came to be linked in the public mind. They once appeared snuggling together on a cover of *Saturday Evening Post*. Famous visitors included the father of the Dionne quintuplets. After he thanked Harbut for the chance to see Man o' War, Will — in whose business prodigious sire records were to be admired — remarked, "I don't so much care about you seeing him, but I sure wanted him to see you!"

Harbut apparently was polite on most occasions, perhaps trying not to scoff whenever he had to say, "No ma'am, he ain't no trotter," but he did not brook any thought that Man o' War was anything less than royalty. When Man o' War happened to be sprawled in his stall and visitors asked that he be gotten up for inspection, Harbut might announce, "Ma'am, that's Man o' War. When he wants to get up, he gets up; when he wants to lie down, he lies down."

Man o' War had come to Kentucky in the winter of 1921 via Maryland. First, though, in what must have been one of the proudest days in Mr. and Mrs. Riddle's lives, he was exhibited to friends and visitors at their beloved Rose Tree Hunt. In their book on Man o' War, Cooper and Treat's recording of the grand trip illustrated the hold Man o' War had on the public, housewives and children as well as sports-loving males:

"Man o' War's immediate destination was Glen Riddle...but it was a slow journey south, for it had no sooner started than it was transformed into a triumphant procession. At every stop along the way, crowds

gathered to see the champion, and he obligingly stuck his proud head out of the van door in answer to their cheers. At last, the caravan reached Pennsylvania. Before going to Glen Riddle, Red and the former show horse, Major Treat, stopped at the Rose Tree Hunt Club in Media, where Mr. Riddle's neighbors and friends had planned a welcome befitting royalty. As the van drew up to the club track, the thousands of people who had been waiting ringed around."

Jack Dempsey was there, a fellow author of the Golden Age of Sport, come to admire one of his comrades in the national arena.

Some three months after his Kenilworth Park Gold Cup swan song, Man o' War arrived in Kentucky. On January 27, 1921, the great Kentucky-bred and soon-to-be monarch made his only appearance at a Kentucky racetrack. He was stabled in Col. E. R. Bradley's barn at the Kentucky Association track in Lexington, on which racing had been conducted for nearly a century. The track by then was shabby and had only another dozen years of existence in front of it, and the strip was sloppy, but Big Red's old friend Clyde Gordon galloped him proudly before an appreciative crowd.

Man o' War stood his first season at stud at Hinata Farm outside Lexington, a farm managed by Miss Elizabeth Daingerfield. [1]

His first stud groom was John Buckner, an accomplished horseman who, according to Bluegrass lore, had had his hands on many a good stallion going back to Domino, Colin, and even Hastings' sire Spendthrift!

Riddle and his wife's niece and nephew-in-law, Kathleen and Walter Jeffords Sr., established Faraway Farm not far from Hinata, and Man o' War was moved there during his second breeding season. None other than Golden Broom was also part of the stallion roster. During the time Man o' War stood at Hinata, Miss Daingerfield purchased and set up Faraway Farm for Riddle. She then continued her management at Faraway until 1930, when she resigned. Hired as manager of Faraway was Harrie B. Scott, who had managed Glen-Helen Farm in Lexington for John Barbee. Riddle had boarded mares at Glen-Helen at least as early as 1918.

Scott's son, Harry, was four years old when Man o' War thus came into his life. Throughout his childhood, he recalls, he was constantly impressed by the line-up of visitors driving through the Faraway gates to see

Man o' War. He remembers famed announcer Clem McCarthy coming to Lexington to do a national radio broadcast of Big Red's twenty-first birthday party.

Man o' War, who filled out to weigh 1,300 pounds in maturity, was exercised regularly during most of the time Harry Scott's father was in charge. Scott recalls that the old temperament began to show itself in the form of rearing up under tack. His father "was afraid the horse would go too far and go over backward, so he gave the fellow who was riding him a rubber hose and said, 'Now, you can feel when Man o' War is about to rear up with you, so you just stand up in the stirrups and pop him between the ears with that rubber hose.' But he said, 'You make sure you don't put an eye out; you put an eye out on that horse and I'll put both of yours out!' "

The Riddles would visit once or twice a year. Mrs. Riddle had knitted saddlecloths for their racehorses for years. She also authored a sentimental little booklet entitled "Man o' War's Talk to His Children," in which she pretended to be the wise old patriarch Big Red writing to his brood about their family history. Harry Scott still cherishes this booklet. Examples of Mrs. Riddle's text:

"...All my children I think are good. Of course, everyone cannot be at the top of his class. We all here won so many stakes that people talk about us, and want our babies. Here in my lovely home I have so many people come to see me from all over the world. They write their names in a big book. It makes me so proud. I just look at them, making believe I am the king of the race track...Even if I am twenty years old, I feel as young as you all do, and love the track, and like hearing about my children making names for themselves...I felt so sorry about (War) Admiral hurting himself in the starting gate of the Belmont. He ran a wonderful race with that awful slice out of his foot... That shows what blood will do..."

This remarkable little personal fantasy was produced privately in 1942. It was the year of Mrs. Riddle's death.

Over the years, Sam Riddle continued to field exalted offers to purchase his horse or to commercialize Big Red's popularity by exhibiting him, at the Chicago World's Fair, for example. On one occasion, W. T. Waggoner of Texas invited Riddle simply to name his own price, to which Riddle gave an elaborate response: "First you go to France and buy the remains of

Napoleon; then you stop by London and pick up the English Crown Jewels; and on the way back purchase the original copy of the Constitution in Washington. And when you get all these back in Texas, then I'll set a price on Man o' War." In other words, Man o' War was not for sale.

The Sire Record

Riddle knew horses and no doubt had great affection for them, Man o' War especially. An intellectual student of breeding, however, he apparently was not. The management of Man o' War was hardly designed to maximize his potential, either commercially or as an influence on the breed. That the stallion succeeded so well and still exists in pedigrees is tribute to the horse more than to how his breeding record was contrived.

First, Riddle decided the horse would be a private stallion, available only to his and the Jeffordses' mares. Then he made a few seasons available to outside mares, first at $2,500 and then up to $5,000. Nor was he known for the quality of the mares he personally presented, or accepted, to the court. (Ogden Phipps, who eventually was able to get to the blood of Man o' War's best son,

with fortuitous results, once quipped to the author that
Riddle's policy seemed to be that "nobody who ever had
a decent mare" got to breed to Man o' War.)

"Mr. Riddle thought Man o' War didn't need good
mares. He thought he was so great he could dominate,"
Scott said. On the other hand, there were times when
Riddle used the opposite ploy. The father's boss, whom
Scott recalls from youth as an "aristocratic, opinion-
ated" figure, would at times use as an excuse not to
grant a requested breeding season that "that mare isn't
good enough for Man o' War."

It was said that Riddle received a letter from the
great botanist Luther Burbank, suggesting that he
make a point of sending young mares to Man o' War.
Own a horse like that, and you get all sorts of advice
from all sorts of quarters.

To some extent, however, this traditional generaliza-
tion about how poor a group of mares Man o' War had
might have been exaggerated. For one thing, early on,
Riddle apparently understood the need to upgrade his
own broodmare band. Miss Daingerfield employed the
help of William Allison, an Englishman who had dealt
with Americans before, notably when advising on the

purchase of more than forty mares for James R. Keene's Castleton Stud. (Miss Daingerfield's father had managed Castleton.) J. A. Estes in *The Blood-Horse* damned and praised (sort of) Allison in a single sentence: The English writer and pedigree expert, Estes wrote, was "best known to his generation for his advocacy of the long since discredited Bruce Lowe Figure Guide, [2] but was a most knowledgeable and able man for all that."

Estes admitted that "the mares selected by Mr. Allison for Riddle and…Jeffords contributed largely to the quick success of Man o' War as a sire." In the stallion's first three crops, totaling fifty-four foals, a dozen were produced from the six mares which had been purchased at Newmarket in 1920 and 1921 in either the name of Allison or Jeffords. The prices of the six mares ranged from $15,750 to $2,730. Among those dozen early Man o' War foals from those mares, three were stakes winners, including American Flag, who was bred and raced by Riddle. Foaled in 1922, American Flag was out of the Roi Herode mare Lady Comfey, who had been purchased at Newmarket by Allison for $4,463.

American Flag, one of only thirteen foals in his sire's first crop, was a moderate stakes winner at two, then in

1925 won three of the prestigious races his own sire had won: the Belmont, Withers, and Dwyer. Also from that first crop came Riddle's Maid At Arms, regarded as co-leader of the three-year-old filly division with Florence Nightingale. Florence Nightingale was a Man o' War filly from the Jeffords' haul and won the Coaching Club American Oaks.

From the next crop, Riddle got another Belmont Stakes winner in the great Crusader, who perhaps was second only to War Admiral among the great stallion's sons. Crusader won two runnings of the Suburban.

Both with the help of Allison and with the benefit of his own program, Jeffords continued as a major benefit to Man o' War and vice versa. His Edith Cavell, from the second crop, matched Florence Nightingale's status as a CCA Oaks winner and co-leader of her division. This was an astounding sequence: Two crops produced two Belmont winners for Riddle and two CCA Oaks winners for Jeffords. If he were wasting the powers of Man o' War, this was a poor era to try to explain as much to Sam Riddle. (Glen Riddle was on a roll. In addition to the Man o' Wars, Riddle owned the top two-year-old filly of 1925 in Friar's Carse, by Friar Rock.)

The fourth crop produced another champion filly for Jeffords in Bateau. A daughter of one of the Allison-advised imports, Escuina, Bateau won the CCA Oaks at three and beat males in the Suburban at four, ranking the equal or superior of contemporary females both years. At that stage, Man o' War had two Belmont winners, three CCA Oaks winners, and the winners of three Suburban Handicaps.

Next came a Kentucky Derby winner in Clyde Van Dusen, one of six stakes winners from his fifth crop of eighteen foals. That crop also included individuals which illustrated Man o' War's hardiness and versatility. One was Annapolis, later a distinguished steeplechase sire, and the other was Hard Tack, whose beloved son Seabiscuit ironically would have his greatest triumph at the expense of War Admiral in the 1938 Pimlico Special. Even more remarkable in terms of versatility was the circumstance of the late 1930s, when Man o' War's sons in action concurrently included American Triple Crown winner War Admiral; English Grand National Steeplechase winner Battleship, still one of the few American-breds to win the world's most famous steeple-chase; Blockade, three-time winner of the demanding timber race, the Maryland Hunt Cup; and Holystone, a consistent winner at high levels in the show ring!

The early returns had been superb, but the figures were not sustainable. From his first five crops, Man o' War got only ninety-two foals, and twenty-six were stakes winners. This came to twenty-eight percent stakes winners from foals, in a breed where three percent is normal, ten percent outstanding, and twenty-five percent attained only by the most exalted sires.

Estes observed in 1947 that, in the next five-year period Man o' War got ninety-one foals, but only half the number of stakes winners. Of the later crops, War Admiral and War Relic appeared, but by and large the decline in quality numbers continued. All told, Man o' War sired 380 foals, of which sixty-four won stakes, still an exceptional seventeen percent. He led the sire list once, in 1926. His progeny earnings exceeded $3 million by 1943, which at that time was more than had been earned collectively by the get of any other stallion.

While leading sires of today are represented by multiples in the sale ring, such was not necessarily the case in Man o' War's time. Only forty-five of his sons and daughters were sold as auction yearlings. One, War Feathers,

topped the Saratoga sales at $50,500 in 1925. Three years later, Broadway Limited sold for $65,000 to rule as the highest-priced of the Man o' Wars. Neither was successful at the racetrack, but War Feathers foaled four stakes winners. The average price for the Man o' Wars at auction was $9,008. Only three won stakes, a seven percent figure well below his overall seventeen percent.

War Admiral and War Relic created a sort of late-crops renaissance. War Admiral, a foal of 1934, was out of Brushup, by Sweep, and was such a smallish, dark bay — unlike Man o' War in the extreme — that Scott recalls Riddle wanted to trade him to Jeffords. Presumably recognizing that it would come up at family dinners and late-night discussions were War Admiral to become a star in Jeffords' colors, the younger man demurred. There were enough family matters that could be sticky without that!

Thus "forced" to keep the colt, Riddle saw War Admiral develop into a highly promising two-year-old, and then in 1937 he allowed trainer George Conway to prepare him for the Kentucky Derby. War Admiral won that classic, as well as the Preakness and Belmont to sweep the noble Triple Crown. He followed his

sire in becoming the leading stallion once (1945).
Also standing for a part of his career at Faraway, War
Admiral sired forty stakes winners, including the won-
derful broodmares Busanda, Searching, and Striking.
His daughter Busher was Horse of the Year at three,
and son Blue Peter was champion at two.

War Admiral was a major link in guaranteeing
the ongoing influence of Big Red insofar as successful producing daughters. On the sire line side, War
Relic has been an important link on to the end of the
20th Century — and likely beyond. A 1938 foal from
Riddle's good filly Friar's Carse, War Relic was inbred
to Fair Play's dam Fairy Gold and had some of the
flash and style of the line. He won the Massachusetts
Handicap, Narragansett Special, and two other stakes
for Riddle at three. War Relic sired only fourteen stakes
winners, but several of them were key figures in subsequent pedigrees. One was the champion Battlefield
and another was the speedy Relic, whose daughter
Relance became a celebrated producer in Europe. War
Relic also sired Intent, from whom springs a flourishing
branch of the sire line today. Intent sired the speedy
Intentionally, in turn the sire of In Reality. In Reality

has been influential both as a sire and broodmare sire. Relaunch, Known Fact, Skywalker, Waquoit, and Bertrando have been among 1990s representatives of the Man o' War sire line tracing to In Reality. The 1990 Kentucky Derby winner and prominent young sire Unbridled traces to In Reality on the bottom side and is thus another of many current animals with at least a bit of the blood of Big Red.

As a sire of broodmares, Man o' War also excelled. With his small numbers due to being, by and large, a private stallion, he had a disadvantage in the sheer numbers (of daughters) game that affects broodmare sire tables. Nevertheless, he ranked second on the broodmare sire list nine times. His more magnificent producing daughters included Boat (five stakes winners), Coquelicot (the Jeffords champion Pavot), Frilette (three stakes winners), Furlough (dam of Kentucky Broodmare of the Year Ace Card), Valkyr (Vagrancy and three other stakes winners), and Salaminia (who figured in the ongoing excellence of pedigree leading to Epsom Derby winner Sir Ivor).

All told, Man o' War's daughters produced 128 stakes winners.

Man o' War began to show signs of heart trouble and was retired from breeding after the 1943 season. Toward the last of Mrs. Riddle's life, her husband had offered that, despite the dangers, he would have the aging Man o' War transported for her to see him one last time. Mrs. Riddle would not ask it.

Riddle understood the hold this horse had on the public and allowed Man o' War's admirers to pay homage until May of 1947, the year the horse turned thirty. Then he felt it necessary to halt the traffic of pilgrims.

Harrie B. Scott, who had kept his own farm while managing Faraway, had left Riddle's employ in 1944 at the time the aging sportsman decided the property should be split into two sections (with the same name). Scott continued to manage the Faraway portion owned by the Jeffordses. (For his son Harry Scott, the wafting melody has never gone silent, for he takes care of the mares owned by the widow of Mr. and Mrs. Walter Jeffords Sr.'s son, Walter Jr.)

Charles Gribbin managed Riddle's portion of Faraway briefly, but returned to the racetrack, and Patrick O'Neill became manager, having worked for Riddle for some years. On November 1, 1947, it fell to O'Neill to issue

the statement that had been dreaded. The Lexington *Herald-Leader* recalled the news as a simple announcement to the Associated Press: "Our big horse just died." Many Lexington residents, who perhaps more than any cradled Man o' War in their hearts as a part of their lives, first got the news when it was announced during a University of Kentucky football game.

Will Harbut had suffered a stroke, and he had died less than a month before.

Veterinarian William R. McGee Sr. had been giving Man o' War sedatives to ease any discomfort. The old horse had seemed to exude a sense of fighting off heart spells, as if the grim reaper was mocking him in the colors of John P. Grier. Finally, he had to accept that Nature was the one rival that could overtake him.

Despite logistical problems, the animal was embalmed and placed in a huge casket which had been constructed some time before in relenting acceptance of the inevitable. The box was lined in the Riddle colors, and Man o' War's body was placed inside (barely fitting, it turned out). About 500 people gathered at Man o' War's funeral, which was broadcast on radio. During the subdued ceremony, Lexington Board of Commerce president Charles Sturgill honored Man o' War as the region's "chief tourist attraction," and breeder A. B. Hancock Jr. said "the name Man o' War is a household word wherever the Thoroughbred is loved." Faraway manager Patrick O'Neill, in his Irish lilt, expressed gratitude for the tributes from around the world, and attending veterinarian McGee noted that, although Mr. Riddle technically owned the horse, in a sense Man o' War "belonged to horsemen everywhere."

Lexington broadcaster Ted Grizzard gave radio listeners a step by step account of the great casket being raised by crane and lowered slowly into the yawning grave. Men saw different things in Man o' War, master of ceremonies Ira Drymon had said, "but one thing they all remembered — that he brought an exultation to their hearts."

Man o' War was buried in a two and a half-acre park, a section of Faraway which Riddle had deeded to Fayette County.

Seven years before, Riddle had asked the international horse sculptor Herbert Haseltine to begin work on a statue. Various matters, including wartime restrictions on materials, had delayed completion. It was not

until 1948 that the 3,000-pound, heroic-sized (twenty hands) figure was transported to Faraway and placed on a granite base over the grave. Along the way, the great Man o' War statue was displayed in the paddock at Belmont Park, where in life he had inspired Abe Hewitt, exasperated James Rowe, and pranced into the memories of thousands.

Haseltine chose to show Man o' War in exaggerated bulges of muscle. "I don't like the statue," Harry Scott admits, and, in truth, it seems the sculptor was seeking mythical emblem as much as specific likeness. No one would question, however, that Haseltine approached the subject with reverence. He recalled having been shown the horse to study and being impressed by his example of that "long, easy walk that presages victory when you see the starters led round the paddock."

Haseltine the artist dealt in bronze, but it was he who also spoke words that recognized both the magic and mystery of Big Red: "There was something that emanated from that noble animal that took my breath away."

Man o' War was always good at that.

MAN O' WAR

EPILOGUE

For The Ages

S amuel D. Riddle outlived Man o' War by less than four years. He suffered a stroke during the final week of 1950 and died on January 8, 1951, at Glen Riddle Farm, his birthplace. He was eighty-nine. Riddle's passing came within two weeks of the death of another famed Turfman, Calumet Farm owner Warren Wright Sr. It took some eight years for the farms, horses, and properties to be sold off by Riddle's estate.

Riddle had continued in racing, although on a lesser scale, and had recently tapped into one of the next of the great bloodline trends when he imported the stallion Somali II, a son of Nasrullah. Riddle, who as a young man often had been referred to as one of the best dressed of his generation, had remained a commanding figure. Around his final birthday, *The Thoroughbred Record* quoted an unnamed source as commenting "He looks like a Roman senator in the days of Cicero and Caesar."

In his interview with Oliver DeWolf for *Daily Racing Form* in 1940, Riddle had mused about death: "You know, when I go to the great beyond, I hope there is some place where the horses can run again."

August Belmont II, breeder of Man o' War, had died at eighty-one in 1924, four years after Man o' War's retirement. His long-time secretary and adviser Adolphe Pons, still in his employ at the end, was the patriarch of a family that today remains involved in racing, at its Country Life Farm in Maryland.

The Belmont legacy and the stable continued to connect with various aspects of American life. Virtually all of Belmont's horses were sold in two large drafts, and it often was assumed that the executors' decisions about whom to sell to were influenced by the fact that both buyers represented families that had lent substantially on the Cape Cod Canal project. (Congress eventually voted to purchase the canal and, in doing so, validate Belmont's vision.) The racehorses were purchased by Averell Harriman, then a young sportsman who was in partnership with George Herbert Walker. They raced together briefly as Log Cabin Stable, and the Belmont horses they acquired included the champion runner and leading sire Chance Play, by Fair Play.

Harriman later left racing and embarked on one of the century's most distinguished careers as an international statesman and presidential adviser as well as serving as governor of New York. His former partner, Walker, became the grandfather of President George Bush.

The Belmont breeding stock was acquired by Joseph E. Widener. The auction where Widener's son, P. A. B. Widener II, was so struck by Fair Play was the sale at which Widener re-sold some of the Belmont horses but turned down a $95,000 bid by Mereworth Farm to retain Fair Play. That moment also was pivotal to another breeder. Marion du Pont Scott, who attended with her father, was already accomplished in the show ring, but had not been involved with Thoroughbreds. She and her father were so impressed by Fair Play that they became interested in the breed which produced him. For a half-century, Mrs. Scott stressed the blood of Fair Play and Man o' War in the successful Thoroughbred breeding and racing program she developed from her historic Montpelier in Virginia. The 1937 English Grand

National Steeplechase winner Battleship, whom she purchased and campaigned, was by Man o' War, and her great broodmare Accra traced to Man o' War and was inbred closely to Fair Play.

Mrs. August Belmont II (née Eleanor Robson) lived to the age of 100. When a stoutish, taciturn older rich man marries a beautiful young Broadway actress, there may be temptation to make certain assumptions about the young lady's long-range agenda. (Belmont had been a widower for a dozen years.) The second Mrs. Belmont, however, never remarried, although she inherited far less than she once might have expected to in earlier years, owing to Belmont's dogged persistence in the Cape Cod Canal effort.

The lady who named Man o' War and saw her husband go overseas in World War I might well have been honored herself by a horse being named something like "Lady o' Valor." Her own efforts on behalf of the war took her on several voyages across the U-boat infested Atlantic as a Red Cross inspector. During marriage to Belmont, her interest in the theater had been expanded by his own devotion to opera. Belmont, however, had to give up his revered Box 4 at the Metropolitan Opera during the Cape Cod Canal struggles, and it was not until 1933 that Mrs. Belmont's finances were such that she even subscribed to the Met again. Thereafter, she became so heavily supportive as an organizer and officer that a handsome portrait of her (painted by Simon Elwes) was placed in the "Belmont Room" at Lincoln Center. Commemorating her 100th birthday in 1978, *Opera News* hailed her "the high priestess of all matters operatic." She died the following year.

Although Mrs. Belmont did not continue in racing after her husband's death, she remained interested in the sport. It was she who contributed the massive bowl still used today as the trophy for the Belmont Stakes; it had been won by her husband's father when Fenian won the 1869 Belmont Stakes. Eleanor Robson Belmont was in the winner's circle to help present the bowl to Sam Riddle after Man o' War's son War Admiral won the Belmont in 1937 — a beautiful lady, in a long patterned dress, with hat, pearls, and gloves.

Many years later, there was a pleasant postscript to all this history when Caveat won the 1983 Belmont in the old scarlet and maroon silks. He was owned by August Belmont IV in partnership with James Ryan and

Robert Kirkham. (August IV once quipped to the author how strange it had been to attend a fete honoring his step-grandmother and, himself nearing seventy, feel like "the youngest one in the room.") Belmont also followed family tradition by serving for a time as chairman of The Jockey Club. He died on July 10, 1995.

Louis Feustel, trainer of Man o' War, returned to training for breeder August Belmont II the year after Big Red was retired. One of his major victories during that term was with Ladkin in one of the International Specials of 1924. Belmont was a strong believer in international racing and had Pierre Wertheimer, the French hero Epinard's owner, as a guest during the series (Epinard was second in all three of the special events.) Feustel remained with the stable after Harriman and Walker purchased the runners, and thus trained Chance Play. Later, he had stints for several owners and lasted for four years with Elizabeth Arden Graham, famed for dismissing trainers in rapid succession.

In 1943, Feustel suffered a fractured pelvis in a freak accident in Miami when a driverless car rolled down an incline and struck him.

Feustel moved to the West Coast, where he trained

Honeymoon and other horses for Harry Warner and also had horses for other owners. He took over a bar named Mickies in Pasadena, California. The bar's decor included some photos of Man o' War, and Feustel on occasion was amused by customers willing to wager that they had been at Churchill Downs the day Big Red "won the Derby!" Feustel died in 1970 in Fremont, Ohio, at the age of eighty-six.

Will Harbut, who died not long before Man o' War's death, had a dozen children, several of whom had jobs with Thoroughbreds. One of his sons, Tom Harbut, exercised War Admiral and War Relic, then in the 1950s for a time was the groom of Nashua — perhaps the top horse in the second-echelon below Man o' War insofar as a Kentucky tourist attraction was concerned.

The portion of **Faraway Farm** which had been owned by Samuel D. Riddle was not sold by his estate until 1958, when the 365 acres brought $255,976. For most of the intervening years, at least a portion of the farm has been known as Man o' War Farm, under various ownerships. In 1997, Mr. and Mrs. Franklin Groves paid $742,500 for a 112-acre tract of the old property. Under Groves' direction, ongoing renovation at the current Man o' War Farm includes refurbishment of the stallion barn built for Man o' War in the late 1930s. Brass name plaques of the stallions of Big Red's era will be affixed to the appropriate stalls.

Man o' War was a hands-down winner when Clem McCarthy polled some forty horsemen as to who were the greatest horses since Longfellow, a few years after Big Red's retirement. In subsequent eras, Man o' War has prevailed. He was voted the best American racehorse of the first half of the 20th Century in an Associated Press poll of sports writers in 1950. In 1999, *The Blood-Horse* magazine convened a panel of racing historians to rank the century's top hundred horses, and Man o' War came out on top. The Associated Press also conducted another poll in 1999, and, again, Man o' War prevailed as the century's best.

The Man o' War Statue eventually was threatened by vandalism and disrepair at its sylvan nook off Faraway Farm. In 1976, the Herbert Haseltine bronze and the remains beneath it were transferred to the new state-owned Kentucky Horse Park north of Lexington. There, in the form of the great bronze, Man o' War stands again in splendid solitude — timeless, serene, supreme.

MAN O' WAR

AFTERWORD

A Century of Legends: Some Burnished, Some Refuted

During the two decades since this volume's first publication, the legend of Man o' War has completed a century. The year 2017 marked the 100th anniversary of the great horse's birth and was the occasion of various commemorative events. One was a ceremony at the Kentucky Horse Park, where the heroic sized statue of the great champion greets visitors. Then, 2018 marked the 100th year since Man o' War's sale as a yearling, and by 2020 the sequence was complete with the centennial of his racing years.

Thoroughbred champions' highlights in those early 21st century decades included the first Triple Crown winner in thirty-seven years, American Pharoah (2015), and the nineteen wins in twenty career starts of the wonderful mare Zenyatta. Still, Man o' War's perch atop all other American racehorses appears secure in the mental and emotional impulses of the American Turf.

For some, of course, the eras and auras of Man o' War are personal. There are those still with us with memories of having visited the great stallion at Faraway Farm in Kentucky, while others had relatives involved in management of his racing career or the farms of his birthplace and years at stud.

Among individual with unique perspectives about Man o' War are Sally Jeffords and Greg Harbut. Ms. Jeffords is a granddaughter of Mr. and Mrs. Walter Jeffords Sr., who were partners with Mr. and Mrs. Samuel D. Riddle in ownership of Faraway Farm. (Mrs. Jeffords Sr. was Mrs. Riddle's niece.) Harbut is a great-grandson of none other than Will Harbut, the sonorous groom of Man o' War who enthralled thousands of visitors with glorious retellings of the great horse's wonders.

Greg Harbut has fashioned his own career in the world of Thoroughbred racing and has also organized efforts to recruit other African-Americans into a sport and business that has lacked inclusion. Harbut is too young to remember Will Harbut or Man o' War, but his grandfather, Tom, had a career similar to Will's and left young Greg with a second-hand, albeit still trenchant, frame of reference. Tom Harbut for a time was the stud groom of Nashua, a 1950s-raced champion who was a bit of a tourist attraction himself, although far from Man o' War status.

One memory the Harbut family has long held is that Will Harbut regarded the way he was depicted as "painful." Yes, Greg testifies, his ancestor was "dedicated to Man o' War beyond an eight-hour day—more like sixteen hours." And yes, there were many moments of pride in how the world's visitors were spellbound by Mr. Harbut's compelling narrative. What was hurtful was the colloquial diction attributed to Will Harbut, who was short on academic education but not unaware of proper patterns of speech. "Mostest hoss that ever wuz" might sound charming to those who have read about it, but not to the gentleman being "quoted." Will Harbut was a spellbinding speaker and entertainer, but he played his role without speaking *that* way.

The fictionalized characterization of Will Harbut latched onto his actual deep baritone, which in some of his relatives augmented reputations for gospel sing-

ing, and paired it with stereotypes that were intended to be complimentary. The late Kent Hollingsworth, editor the *The Blood-Horse*, in 1970 described Harbut as an "epic poet" based on contemporary accounts he had read.

Somewhere along the way, however, the distinguished gentleman was given vocal characteristics by writers thinking they were extolling him. The ironies are well known in literature by white Americans. The Atlanta journalist and author Joel Chandler Harris keenly supported regional and racial reconciliation, and yet his lovingly told Bre'r Rabbit stories embraced a form of African-American speech that came to be seen as anything but respectful. Similar in effect was the 1920s blockbuster debut of the Broadway musical *Show Boat*, based on Edna Ferber's novel. For Will Harbut, the lampoon posing as veneration was not something seen in books and movies. They were difficult, painful, and daily parts of his own life.

A vigorous scion of the family in the 21st century, Greg Harbut has fashioned his own career as a bloodstock agent and owner. His work for the prominent Yoshida family of Japan includes the acquisition of many of the sixteen grade 1 winners Harbut Bloodstock has acquired. "I am known as 'the mare man,'" Harbut said, not in jest. "When a major mare is for sale, they (sellers) tend to let me know."

Recently, Harbut's efforts on behalf of increasing the Turf's opportunities for African-Americans include launching a series of lectures at Wilberforce University. Harbut's series at the traditionally all-Black college in Dayton, Ohio, introduces to young students the many and varied jobs and careers involved in the multi-faceted world of Thoroughbred racing. In addition to hands on horsemanship roles, they include corporate positions with racetracks, bloodstock agencies, regulatory agencies, support services, and Thoroughbred organizations.

For Sally Jeffords, the link to Man o' War also is a matter of family life. She used to be aware that her father, Walter Jeffords Jr.—a grand horseman she admired—might at times be foxhunting on a son or grandson of Man o' War, and she was proud that Man o' War is in the pedigree of her mother's Hall of Fame steeplechaser Lonesome Glory. Her memorabilia include a Percy Earl portrait of Man o' War and copies of

the sentimental booklet her great-aunt, Mrs. Samuel Riddle Riddle, penned as if written by Man o' War himself. These might be matters for history books or museums, but they are also, well, a comfortable part of her family life and memory.

Ms. Jeffords also has reached out to create her own personal stamp on her Man o' War heritage. She has been involved as a breeder and owner in the past, largely with steeplechase horses, and she currently is chair of the Collections and Exhibitions Committee of the National Museum of Racing in Saratoga, NY.

Upset: Fact and Fiction

Just as the aura of Will Harbut misses the mark in terms of accuracy in one aspect, so does a popular tale involving Man o' War's only defeat. So stunning, and remembered, was Man o' War's one loss—to a horse named Upset—that it was appealing to ascribe to that moment in 1919 the beginning of the word "upset" being used for any surprising sporting event result. Lexicographers and etymologists probably always thought the tale too good to be true, but it was popular. Then, in 2002 a wordsmith researcher named

George Thompson applied modern online text-tracking technology to the subject. Using the *New York Times* databases, Thompson found sports-event usage of "upset" as a verb as far back as 1865 and as a noun at least back to 1877.

So, the result of the 1919 Sanford Memorial might have altered history, but not dictionaries.

An Enduring Bloodline

Meanwhile, the legacy of Man o' War as a continuing presence in pedigrees has crossed into another century. In the narrow context of the male-line descent, Tiznow, the two-time Breeders' Cup Classic winner, was retired from the stud in 2020, but has seven sons advertised as stallions for 2021. Tiznow harks back eight generations to Man o' War, one more than Honour and Glory, also represented by a few male line descendants.

A horse does not appear only in the male line of pedigrees, of course, and the Man o' War connection through Tiznow had a classic meeting of centuries in 2020. Tiz the Law, son of a Tiznow mare, won the historic Belmont Stakes—just as Man o' War had won the

classic an even 100 years earlier!

Another pleasing aspect of Man o' War's legacy is that the barn where he was housed through much of his stallion career is still extant, and well preserved. Custodian of that jewel of history is Greg Goodman, whose Mt. Brilliant Farm includes a portion of the old Faraway Farm. Himself a polo devotee as well as successful Thoroughbred breeder, Goodman launched a renovation project that preserves the four-stall barn in a condition very close to its appearance in the 1930s and 1940s. On occasion, Goodman has allowed a charitable organization to hold a lunch in the old barn as a fund raiser—a unique toasting and touching between species and eras.

Man o' War

ch. c. 1917, by Fair Play (Hastings)–Mahubah, by Rock Sand
Own.– Glen Riddle Farm
Br.– Mr. August Belmont (Ky)
Tr.– Louis Feustel

Lifetime record: 21 20 1 0 $249,465

12Oct20- 4Knw	fst	$1\frac{1}{4}$	:46^{2} 1:11^{4} 1:37^{2} 2:03	3↑ Ken Park Gold Cup 75k	2 1	1^{2}	1^{5}	1^{6}	1^{7}	Kummer C	120 w	*.05	132-03	Man o' War120^{7}Sir Barton126	Never extended	2
18Sep20- 5HdG	fst	$1\frac{1}{16}$	:23 :47^{3} 1:11^{3} 1:44^{4}	Potomac H 10k	4 1	$1^{1\frac{1}{2}}$	1^{1}	$1^{1\frac{1}{2}}$	$1^{1\frac{1}{2}}$	Kummer C	138 w	*.15	101-16	Man o' War138$^{1\frac{1}{2}}$Wildair108^{15}Blazes104.5^{2}	Easing late	4
11Sep20- 4Bel	fst	$1\frac{1}{2}$	:49^{3} 1:14^{1} 2:03^{2} 2:28^{4}	3↑ Jockey Club 6.8k	2 1	1^{5}	1^{8}	1^{12}	1^{15}	Kummer C	118 w	*.01	117-02	Man o' War118^{15}Damask118	Under a pull	2
4Sep20- 4Bel	fst	$1\frac{5}{8}$	:47^{4} 2:03^{3} 2:28^{4} 2:40^{4}	Lawrence Realizatn 16k	2 1	1^{20}	1^{30}	1^{50}	1^{100}	Kummer C	126 w	*.01	134-00	Man o' War126^{100}Hoodwink116	Restrained at end	2
21Aug20- 4Sar	fst	$1\frac{1}{4}$	:46^{3} 1:10 1:35^{3} 2:01^{4}	Travers 12k	1 1	1^{2}	1^{4}	1^{4}	$1^{2\frac{1}{2}}$	Schuttinger A	129 w	*.22	102-08	Mano'War129$^{2\frac{1}{2}}$Upset123^{7}JohnP.Grier115	Restrained in str	3
7Aug20- 4Sar	fst	$1\frac{3}{16}$	:48^{1} 1:12^{4} 1:37^{4} 1:56^{3}	Miller 5.7k	2 1	$1^{1\frac{1}{2}}$	1^{3}	1^{4}	1^{6}	Sande E	131 w	*.03	97-09	Mano'War131^{6}Donnacona119^{4}KingAlbert114	Never extended	3
10Jly20- 4Aqu	fst	$1\frac{1}{8}$	:46 1:09^{3} 1:36 1:49^{1}	Dwyer 5.5k	1 1	1^{hd}	1^{hd}	$1^{\frac{1}{2}}$	$1^{1\frac{1}{2}}$	Kummer C	126 w	*.20	101-08	Man o' War126$^{1\frac{1}{2}}$John P. Grier108	Hard ridden,drew away	2
22Jun20- 4Jam	gd	1	:25^{3} :49 1:14^{1} 1:41^{3}	Stuyvesant H 4.5k	1 1	1^{4}	1^{7}	1^{8}	1^{8}	Kummer C	135 w	*.01	86-13	Man o' War135^{8}Yellow Hand103	Eased final ⅛	2
12Jun20- 4Bel	fst	$1\frac{3}{8}$	2:14^{1}	Belmont 9.2k	1 1	1^{2}	1^{7}	1^{12}	1^{20}	Kummer C	126 w	*.04	116-10	Man o' War126^{20}Donnacona126	Taken up final $\frac{1}{16}$	2
29May20- 4Bel	fst	1	:24 :47^{1} 1:11 1:35^{4}	Withers 5.8k	2 1	$1^{1\frac{1}{2}}$	1^{2}	1^{2}	1^{2}	Kummer C	118 w	*.14	104-10	Man o' War118^{2}Wildair118^{12}David Harum118	Won under pull	3
18May20- 4Pim	fst	$1\frac{1}{8}$	:47^{3} 1:12^{2} 1:38^{1} 1:51^{3}	Preakness 29k	7 1	$1^{1\frac{1}{2}}$	1^{4}	1^{2}	$1^{1\frac{1}{2}}$	Kummer C	126 w	*.80	97-10	Man o' War126$^{1\frac{1}{2}}$Upset122^{5}Wildair114^{5}	Speed in reserve	9
13Sep19- 3Bel	fst	6f-Str	1:11^{3}	Futurity 31k	8 2	$3^{1\frac{1}{2}}$	$1^{\frac{1}{2}}$	1^{2}	$1^{2\frac{1}{2}}$	Loftus J	127 w	*.50	85-21	Mano'War127$^{2\frac{1}{2}}$JohnP.Grier117^{4}Dominiqu122^{nk}	Won easing up	10
30Aug19- 3Sar	sl	6f	:23 :47 1:13	Hopeful 29k	3 4	2^{2}	2^{1}	1^{5}	1^{4}	Loftus J	130 w	*.45	87-14	Man o' War130^{4}Cleopatra112^{4}Constancy124^{2}	Easily	8
23Aug19- 3Sar	fst	6f	:22^{3} :46^{2} 1:12	Grand Union Hotel 9.8k	2 3	1^{hd}	1^{3}	1^{3}	1^{1}	Loftus J	130 w	*.55	92-08	Man o' War130^{1}Upset125^{4}Blazes122$^{\frac{1}{2}}$	Eased final 16th	10
13Aug19- 4Sar	fst	6f	:23^{1} :46^{4} 1:11^{1}	Sanford Memorial 4.9k	6 5	$4^{1\frac{1}{2}}$	3^{2}	$3^{1\frac{1}{2}}$	$2^{\frac{1}{2}}$	Loftus J	130 w	*.55	95-09	Upst115$^{\frac{1}{2}}$Mno'Wr130^{3}GoldnBroom130^{2}	Slow start,gaining	7
2Aug19- 3Sar	fst	6f	:23 :47^{1} 1:12^{2}	U S Hotel 9.8k	8 1	1^{3}	1^{3}	1^{4}	1^{2}	Loftus J	130 w	*.90	90-13	Man o' War130^{2}Upset115^{1}Homely112^{1}	Eased final 16th	10
5Jly19- 3Aqu	fst	6f	:23^{3} :47^{2} 1:13	Tremont 5.8k	2 2	1^{1}	1^{1}	$1^{1\frac{1}{2}}$	1^{1}	Loftus J	130 w	*.10	90-12	Man o' War130^{1}Ralco115^{20}Ace of Aces112	Never extended	3
23Jun19- 3Aqu	fst	5f	1:01^{3}	Hudson 3.4k	2 1	$1^{\frac{1}{2}}$	1^{1}	1^{1}	$1^{1\frac{1}{2}}$	Loftus J	130 w	*.10e	83-12	Mano'War130$^{1\frac{1}{2}}$VioletTip109^{4}Shoal115^{12}	Broke thru barrier	5
21Jun19- 3Jam	gd	$5\frac{1}{2}$f	:23^{1} :47^{3} 1:00^{1} 1:06^{3}	Youthful 4.8k	4 3	1^{1}	1^{2}	1^{4}	$1^{2\frac{1}{2}}$	Loftus J	120 w	*.50	92-09	Mno'War120$^{2\frac{1}{2}}$OnWtch108^{2}LdyBrumml105^{10}	Easing final 16th	4
9Jun19- 4Bel	sl	$5\frac{1}{2}$f-Str	1:05^{3}	Keene Mem 5.2k	3 2	$2^{\frac{1}{2}}$	$3^{\frac{3}{4}}$	3^{1}	1^{3}	Loftus J	115 w	*.70	91-17	Man o' War115^{3}On Watch115$^{\frac{1}{2}}$Anniversary115^{4}	Drew away	6
6Jun19- 6Bel	fst	5f-Str	:59	Md Sp Wt	7 1	2^{nk}	$2^{\frac{1}{2}}$	1^{3}	1^{6}	Loftus J	115 w	*.60	83-18	Man o' War115^{6}Retrieve112$^{\frac{1}{2}}$Neddam115^{4}	Easily	7

Past Performances courtesy Daily Racing Form LLC © 1999, reprinted from the book "Champions" (DRF Press)

References

Introduction

1. Page Cooper and Roger Treat. *Man o' War*. (New York: Julian Messner, Inc., 1950), from foreword.

Chapter 1

1. Abram S. Hewitt, *Sire Lines*. (Lexington, KY: The Blood-Horse, 1977)
2. Abram S. Hewitt, *Great Breeders and their Methods*. (Lexington, KY: Thoroughbred Publishers, 1982)
3. Bernard Livingston, *Their Turf*. (New York: Arbor House, 1973)
4. Ibid.
5. Kent Hollingsworth, *The Kentucky Thoroughbred*. (Lexington, KY: University of Kentucky Press, 1976)
6. Ibid.
7. Sam Hildreth and James R. Crowell, *The Spell of the Turf*. (Philadelphia: J. B. Lippincott Co., 1926)
8. J. A. Estes, "Man o' War." *The Blood-Horse*, Nov. 8, 1947, p. 342.
9. Kent Hollingsworth, *The Kentucky Thoroughbred*.
10. Edward Hotaling, *They're Off, Horse Racing at Saratoga*. (Syracuse, NY: Syracuse University Press, 1995)
11. Abram S. Hewitt, *Sire Lines*.
12. Mrs. Hutchison has fond memories of Sam Riddle, who, when learning she was the daughter of a friend, Mary King, insisted that she stay at his Faraway Farm when she first went to Lexington to buy horses. Riddle had his farm manager assist in what turned out to be early acquisitions for Mrs. Hutchison's and her first husband's successful North Cliff Farm.

Chapter 2

1. J. A. Estes, "Man o' War." *The Blood-Horse*, Nov. 8, 1947, p. 342.
2. Abram S. Hewitt, *Great Breeders and Their Methods*.
3. Wayne Capps, "The Man Who Will Always See Red," from *Turf & Sport Digest*, 1958.

4. Despite his low initial status when surrounded by classic winners in the stud's history, the speedy Phalaris founded the predominant sire line of the 20th Century, whose various representatives include Nearco, Nasrullah, Royal Charger, Bold Ruler, Turn-to, Northern Dancer, Native Dancer, Raise a Native, and Mr. Prospector.

5. Abram S. Hewitt, *Sire Lines*.

6. Kent Hollingsworth, *The Great Ones*. (Lexington, KY: The Blood-Horse, 1970)

7. Dorothy Ours, *Chain Lightning: The True Legend of Man o' War*. (unpublished)

8. P. A. B. Widener II, *Without Drums*. (New York: G. P. Putnam's Sons, 1940)

9. British Bloodstock Agency, *Bloodstock Breeders' Review*, 1920.

10. Dan M. Bowmar III, *Giants of the Turf*. (Lexington, KY: The Blood-Horse, 1960)

11. Sam Hildreth and James R. Crowell, *The Spell of the Turf*.

12. In recent times, Masda has appeared in the direct female lineage of several stakes winners, including Academy Award, a son of Secretariat. Additionally, she was the fourth dam of Prove Out, he the broodmare sire of the champion international racer and producer Miesque.

13. In *Without Drums*, P. A. B. Widener II expressed the sweet, but naive thought that, "Though we have never owned Man o' War, we hope that when he dies, he, too, will be buried at (our) Elmendorf."

Chapter 3

1. J. K. M. Ross, *Boots and Saddles*. (New York: E. P. Dutton & Co., 1956)

2. In the anthology *The Fireside Book of Horse Racing* (Simon and Schuster), editor David F. Woods attributed the *Times* report to Fred Van Ness.

3. Edward Hotaling, *They're Off: Horse Racing at Saratoga*.

Chapter 4

1. Obituary of Samuel D. Riddle, *The Thoroughbred Record*, 1951.

2. Walter Vosburgh, *Racing In America, 1866-1921*. (New York: The Jockey Club, 1922)

3. Lexington *Herald-Leader*, July 27, 1997.

4. The strictures of the Jersey Act applied to breeding and did not preclude horses from competing in England.

Chapter 5

1. Recalling that Mrs. Edward Kane had been managing director of Nursery Stud when Man o' War was raised there, it might seem that at least some in the Kentucky Thoroughbred businesses were well ahead of their time in terms of management opportunities for women!

2. A system of evaluating pedigrees on the basis of female families tracing to specific taproot individuals.

Index

163

Photo Credits

Cover photo: (Keeneland-Cook)

Page 1: Man o' War as a suckling (The Blood-Horse); as a yearling (The Blood-Horse); at two with Loftus, Riddle, and Feustel (The Blood-Horse)

Page 2: August Belmont II (New York Racing Association Photo); with Louis Feustel (NYRA Photo); with Sam Hildreth (NYRA Photo)

Page 3: Samuel D. Riddle (The Blood-Horse); with his wife, Elizabeth (Keeneland-Cook); with Man o' War (Brownie Leach Photo)

Page 4: Fair Play (The Blood-Horse); Mahubah (The Blood-Horse); Rock Sand (McClure Collection); Hastings (The Blood-Horse)

Page 5: Sanford Stakes (Keeneland-Cook); John Loftus (Keeneland-Cook)

Page 6: Belmont Futurity post parade (NYRA Photo); Belmont Futurity, J. Loftus up (Keeneland-Cook); Clarence Kummer (Keeneland-Cook)

Page 7: Man o' War, 1920 Belmont Stakes (Jerry Cooke Collection); Man o' War (Keeneland-McClure)

Page 8-9: Travers Stakes (Keeneland-Cook); Dwyer Stakes (Keeneland-Cook); Sir Barton Match Race (Sutcliffe Pictures)

Page 10: Man o' War with men (Keeneland-McClure); Man o' War with groom John Buckner (Keeneland-McClure)

Page 11: Man o' War under saddle (Mack Hughes); Man o' War birthday party (Widener Collection)

Page 12: Man o' War with Will Harbut (James W. Sames III photos)

Page 13: War Admiral (Morgan Photo Service); Clyde Van Dusen (Churchill Downs); War Relic (The Blood-Horse); Blockade (Bert Morgan)

Page 14: Maid At Arms (Keeneland-Cook); Bateau (Keeneland-Cook); Florence Nightingale (Keeneland-Cook); Unbridled (John C. Engelhardt)

Page 15: Faraway Farm barn and sign (Barbara D. Livingston); Man o' War burial (James W. Sames III)

Page 16: Man o' War funeral (James W. Sames III); Statue unveiling (Keeneland Library)

Edward **L. Bowen** is the author of more than twenty books on Thoroughbred racing history. He was a staff member of the weekly trade publication *The Blood Horse* for some thirty years, including seventeen as managing editor and five as editor-in-chief. He was also editor of *The Canadian Horse* for two years. Bowen served as president of the Grayson-Jockey Club Research Foundation from 1994 through 2018. Bowen has received various honors within the world of Thoroughbred and sports journalism and authorship, including an Eclipse Award for magazine writing, the Charles Engelhard Award from the Kentucky Thoroughbred Association, the Old Hilltop Award from Pimlico Race Course, the Walter Haight Award from the National Turf Writers Association, and the gold medal designation in Foreword's sports category.